# AN ESSAY ON ORIGINAL GENIUS

# AN ESSAY

## ON

# ORIGINAL GENIUS

### AND ITS VARIOUS MODES OF EXERTION
### IN PHILOSOPHY AND THE FINE ARTS,
### PARTICULARLY IN POETRY
(1767)

BY

## WILLIAM DUFF

A FACSIMILE REPRODUCTION

EDITED WITH AN INTRODUCTION

BY

## JOHN L. MAHONEY

GAINESVILLE, FLORIDA

SCHOLARS' FACSIMILES & REPRINTS

1964

SCHOLARS' FACSIMILES & REPRINTS

1605 N.W. 14TH AVENUE

GAINESVILLE, FLORIDA, U.S.A.

HARRY R. WARFEL, GENERAL EDITOR

L.C. CATALOG CARD NUMBER: 64-10669

MANUFACTURED IN THE U.S.A.

TYPESETTING BY J. N. ANZEL, INC.

LITHOPRINTING BY EDWARDS BROTHERS

BINDING BY UNIVERSAL-DIXIE BINDERY

# INTRODUCTION

One of the most significant aspects of the emerging romanticism of middle and later eighteenth century English literary theory was the pronounced concern with the operations of the human mind, with the effect of art on the reader or spectator, and with those means of achieving this particular effect. Accompanying this new concern is a growing minimization of the criticism of literature on traditional and formalistic grounds or in accordance with certain preestablished rules and formulae. Artists and critics alike reveal an increasing weariness with moral strictures embodied in the familiar couplet framework, with the notion that mere regularity is a quality to be prized. They bring to their writing an increased awareness that sensation and imagination have valid places in any consideration of man's sources of knowledge, that life and literature are more than purely rational activities, that strong emotion and freedom from rules are often foundations for the production of great art. As Walter J. Bate contends in *From Classic to Romantic,* such tendencies are indicative that "critical theory followed the lead of formal empirical psychology, and turned upon the mind itself, hoping, through psychological analysis, to discover at least some common principle of human feeling and human reaction by which some standard of taste could be developed."

v

Genius, imagination, taste, and sublimity become key themes in literature and criticism of the period, particularly in that body of literary theory produced by a group of Scottish writers that includes Adam Smith, Henry Home, Lord Kames, Alexander Gerard, and William Duff. Documents like Smith's *Theory of Moral Sentiments* (1759), Gerard's *Essay on Taste* (1759), and Kames' *Elements of Criticism* (1762) were important forces in furthering the subjective drift of British criticism fifty years before Wordsworth and Coleridge.

William Duff's *Essay on Original Genius* (1767), a facsimile of which is offered in this volume, is certainly one of the most important and interesting documents of the Scottish school. Duff was born in 1732, was ordained to the ministry on October 8, 1755, and appointed to the parish of Shenbucket in Aberdeenshire. He was married and the father of two sons and four daughters. In February of 1774 he was nominated as minister of Foveran in Aberdeenshire, built a new church in 1794, and died as father of the synod in 1815.

In addition to the *Essay on Original Genius*, Duff published a variety of writings during his career. In 1770 he wrote a sequel to the *Essay* called *Critical Observations on the Writings of the Most Celebrated Original Geniuses in Poetry*. His *The History of Rhedi, the Hermit of Mount Ararat, An Oriental Tale* appeared in 1773. His moral and religious works include *Sermons on Several Occasions* (1786), *Letters on the Intellectual and Moral Character of Women* (1807), and *The Last Address of a Clergyman in the Decline of Life* (1814).

It is the *Essay on Original Genius*, however, which stands as his most famous work, revealing his wise knowledge of classical and contemporary literature, and particularly his interest in psychology and the psychological approach to the arts. Although focusing on the central idea of what constitutes genius, it is most interesting to observe how this focus suggests a whole approach to art and criticism, an approach that will receive its most eloquent statement in the romantic criticism of Coleridge and Hazlitt.

For Duff genius is distinguished almost exclusively by imagination, by originality as opposed to mere capacity. It is neither uniform nor periodical in its appearance, flourishing most often in early and uncultivated periods of society before the maturity and cultivation that accompany reason. Imagination is not the "decaying sense" of Hobbes, not the mere picture-making faculty which serves to adorn the truth, not the mirror-like faculty of the Augustans, concepts which had pervaded the rationalistic psychology of the previous age. It is rather, to borrow M.A. Abrams' term, the lamp, the faculty which "by its plastic power of inventing new associations of ideas, and of combining them with infinite variety, is enabled to present a creation of its own." It is not simply an adorner, but a revealer. Since it finds "no objects in the visible creation sufficiently marvelous and new, or which can give full scope to the exercise of its power," it "naturally bursts into the ideal world." Imagination for Duff "calls shadowy substances and unreal objects into existence"; far from merely reproducing, it transforms and illuminates the objects of experience.

Wit and humor are not to be equated with imagination because they are not creative; they possess neither the range nor the vigor of the greater faculty. The achievements of wit are fanciful. It is "a quickness and readiness of fancy in assembling such ideas as lay latent in the mind, till the combining power of association, with the assistance of the retentive faculty, calls them forth, by the suggestion of some distant, but perhaps corresponding circumstance." Its products are smart repartees, ingenious conceits, fanciful allusions, and brilliant sentiments. In Duff's fundamental distinction can be seen a striking anticipation of Coleridge's romantic separation of the fancy, as a kind of arbitrary drawing together of things that lie distant, from the creative imagination as a magical faculty of the mind which, when strongly excited, generates and produces a form of its own. It is Coleridge's theory of imagination that dominated nineteenth century literary theory and has persisted in a great deal of contemporary criticism.

It is only when wit is accompanied by a rich and varied fund of invention that it can lay claim to genius. The rare exception is a poem like Pope's "Rape of the Lock" "in which, though the machinery of the Sylphs is not the mere creation of the Poet's fancy, yet the particular nature and employment of those wonderful aerial beings is altogether his own fiction." In Duff's opinion Pope, like Shakespeare, had undoubtedly gained the distinction of being a man of genius and wit.

Shakespeare, as the poet of imagination, is the great exemplar of genius. He is everywhere to be distinguished from the poet of wit and fancy which are lesser faculties in Duff's psychology. "Every man of Great Wit," he argues in a manner reminiscent of the later distinctions of Wordsworth and Coleridge, "will not be a Great Genius, nor

will every man of Great Genius be a Great Wit.
These qualities do not always exist together. Thus
Swift was not a Genius ... nor Ossian a Wit. ...
Genius, whose ideas are vivid and comprehensive,
is not always united with wit, whose conceptions
are quick and lively but frequently superficial."

Duff's *Essay*, in its concern with the freedom
that characterizes genius and with nature in its
grander manifestations, sheds a great deal of val-
uable light on new trends in the poetry and prose
of the later eighteenth century. Its constant praise
of the natural over the artificial, the imagination
over reason, and emotion over restraint is sympto-
matic of the movement from neoclassic to romantic
in the age.

I would like to acknowledge my deep apprecia-
tion to the Harvard University Library for permis-
sion to make this facsimile of Duff's *Essay*. I would
also like to thank Professor Harry Warfel, general
editor of *Scholars' Facsimiles and Reprints,* for his
assistance and encouragement during the prepara-
tion of this work.

JOHN L. MAHONEY

*Boston College*

# AN ESSAY

## ON

# ORIGINAL GENIUS;

### AND ITS

### VARIOUS MODES OF EXERTION

### IN

## PHILOSOPHY

### AND THE

## FINE ARTS,

### PARTICULARLY IN

## POETRY.

---

*Nullius addictus jurare in verba magistri.* HORAT.

---

LONDON:

Printed for Edward and Charles. Dilly in the *Poultry,*
near the *Mansion-House.*

---

M DCC LXVII.

# ADVERTISEMENT.

TO explain the nature of GE-
NIUS, to point out its effential ingredients, to fhew the refpective
and the combined efficacy of thofe
ingredients in compofition, as well as
in the refearches of Science and the
inventions or improvements of Art,
is the principal defign of the following Effay. It is of little importance
for the Reader to know what were
the Author's motives for its publica-
tion, or how it comes to be offered
to the Public in its prefent form.
Thus far however it may not be im-

proper

proper to acquaint him, that though
the Author had at firſt reſolved to
confine his views to the conſideration
of the ingredients, exertions, and effects of ORIGINAL POETIC GE-
NIUS alone, he was, upon maturer
deliberation, inclined to extend his
proſpects; and, by taking a more extenſive ſurvey of his ſubject, was deſirous to render the deſign of the
Eſſay more complete. He acknowledges likewiſe, that he was partly led
on to this method of proſecuting his
plan by gradual and almoſt imperceptible ſteps; finding his ſubject
growing upon him while he contemplated it nearly, and new proſpects
opening themſelves to the imagination,
in proportion to the progreſs he had
made. As he had not therefore fixed
his

his attention wholly on any particular fpecies of Genius, fo as to exclude
altogether the confideration of any
other fpecies; and as he hath taken
occafion to explain both the general
nature and the peculiar modifications
of this quality, as exerted in the various provinces of Imagination, with
various degrees of energy; he refolved
to intitle his performance AN ESSAY
ON ORIGINAL GENIUS; which
title he thought would be moft expreffive of its defign, and include
under it the feveral kinds of Genius
treated of in the courfe of the following Differtation.  At the fame
time it cannot but be obferved, that
the Author hath kept the main object
of his attention principally in his eye;
that he hath more particularly explain-

A 3                                    ed

ed the nature, as well as marked the indications and efforts of ORIGINAL POETIC GENIUS, than thofe of any other mode of this quality; and that the remarks which he hath made upon its other modes and degrees, are like fo many lines meeting in one central point, to which the eye is directed as the termination of its profpect.

IT will likewife be obferved, that in this view the Firft Book may very properly be confidered as an Introduction to the Second, in which the fubject is branched out into its various parts, and more particularly difcuffed. In the firft fection of the former, the objects and ingredients of Genius are inquired into, as well as the efficacy of thofe ingredients in compofition;

seldom appear in a very high degree in cultivated life; of which he hath likewife attempted to affign the reafons.

SUCH is the general plan of the Effay now fubmitted, with the utmoft deference, to the judgment and candor of the Public. The Author might avail himfelf of the ordinary practice of foliciting an indulgence to the faults of his performance, and he is fenfible that in many inftances he ftands in need of it; but as he does not think it reafonable to expect an indulgence to faults, which either a more accurate examination of his Work would have qualified him to correct; or which, if incorrigible, a proper fenfe of his own abilities would have enabled him to difcern; he is under a neceffity of appealing

pealing to the impartial judgment of
his Readers, however difadvantageous
that appeal may be to himfelf; confcious as he is, that the utmoft an
Author can hope for, is a candid examination of his compofitions, and
an equitable decifion concerning their
genuine merit.

He is at the fame time well aware,
that in an Essay on Original Genius,
Originality of Sentiment will naturally,
and may, no doubt, juftly be expected ;
and that where this is altogether want-
ing, no other excellence can fupply the
defect.   This obfervation, it muft be
confeffed, furnifhes a very fevere teft
for determining the merit of the following production , and indeed the
Author is not a little apprehenfive of
the

the iffue of a ftrict examination. In the
mean time, though he has already pre-
cluded himfelf from the ufual pleas to
indulgence, he may at leaft be allowed
to fuggeft the difficulty of the attempt,
as fome kind of apology for the defects
in the execution. The far greater
number even of thofe who pretend to
be poffeffed of learning and intellectual
accomplifhments, being neither capable
nor willing to think for themfelves on
any fubject, are contented to adopt the
fentiments of perfons of fuperior abilities, that are circulated in books or
in converfation, and echoed from
mouth to mouth. It may likewife
be remarked, that it is frequently no
eafy matter to diftinguifh the fentiments that are derived from the
fources above-mentioned, from thofe
that

that are properly original, and are
the result of invention and reflection
united together. A casual coincidence
of sentiment will sometimes happen,
where not the least imitation was intended; and when this is the case,
the Author, in whose compositions it
is found, may as justly affert his claim
to Originality, as if no such coincidence had ever existed.

To these considerations, which will
in several instances at least account for
an accidental SIMILARITY, and even
SAMENESS of sentiments with those
of others, suppofing them to have
happened in some parts of the following Essay, the Author of it begs leave
to subjoin a caution to his Readers:
It is, that they would not expect to
meet

meet with original fentiments in thofe
parts of this Effay, where it is fcarce
poffible they fhould be difcovered.
Thus, for inftance, in enumerating the
ingredients, pointing out the objects,
or illuftrating the efforts of Genius,
there is very little fcope afforded for
any new track of thought; and thofe
who would form juft opinions of the
above-mentioned articles, muft think
as the beft Authors who have gone
before them have done upon the fame
fubjects.   Other parts of the following Treatife certainly afford fufficient
fcope for original fentiments; and if
the Author has not been fo happy as
to ftrike out fome of thefe, he hath
indeed laboured in vain, and very
much failed in the attainment of his
propofed end.

I<small>F</small>

I F he hath difcovered a vein of original fentiment in any part of the following Work, it will probably appear in thofe fections wherein he has confidered the conneftions betwixt GENIUS, WIT, and HUMOUR; traced the mutual influence of IMAGINATION on TASTE, and of TASTE on IMAGI‑ NATION; explained the different modifications, degrees, and exertions of ORIGINAL GENIUS, as appearing in PHILOSOPHY, POETRY, and the other fine Arts ; pointed out the PERIOD of SOCIETY moft favourable to the Difplay of ORIGINAL POETIC GENIUS in particular, and produced various arguments in fupport of the pofition he hath advanced. In what degree Originality of Sentiment is really difcovered on the above-mentioned fub‑ jects,

jects, muſt be left to the determina-
tion of the intelligent and impartial
Reader. The Author, for his own
part, can at leaſt declare, that he is
not conſcious of having borrowed his
obſervations on theſe ſubjects from
the Writings of any other perſon whatever.

SHOULD the volume now offered to
the Public, be ſo happy as to obtain its
approbation, another will ſoon ſuc-
ceed; in which the principal deſign
of the preſent volume will be farther
purſued, wherein the obſervations on
ORIGINAL POETIC GENIUS contained
in it, will be exemplified by quotations from the Works of the greateſt
original Geniuſes in Poetry, whether
ancient or modern.

ON

O N the other hand, if the prefent volume fhould unhappily fall under the public cenfure, the Author will not be fo unreafonable as to remon-ftrate or complain; for though the public judgment is not infallible, it will for the moft part be found to be more juft, as it certainly will be more impartial, than the opinion of any Writer concerning the merit of his own productions.

THE

# THE
# CONTENTS

## BOOK I.

OF the Nature, Properties, and Indications of GENIUS; and of the various Modes of Exertion, - *Page* 1

### SECTION I.

Of the Objects and Ingredients of GENIUS; and of the Efficacy of those Ingredients united in Composition, - - - 3

### SECTION II.

Of the usual Indications of GENIUS, - 27

### SECTION III.

Of the Connection betwixt GENIUS, WIT, and HUMOUR, - - - - - 46

### SECTION IV.

Of the mutual Influence of IMAGINATION on TASTE, and of TASTE on IMAGINATION, considered

---

AN

# AN ESSAY ON GENIUS.

## BOOK I.

### OF THE

NATURE, PROPERTIES, and INDICATIONS

OF

## GENIUS;

AND OF ITS

VARIOUS MODES of EXERTION.

# SECTION I.

## OF THE

## OBJECTS AND INGREDIENTS

### OF

# GENIUS;

### AND OF THE

## EFFICACY of thofe INGREDIENTS

### UNITED IN

# COMPOSITION.

IT muſt have occurred to every one who has ſurveyed, with an ordinary degree of attention, the unequal diſtribution of natural talents among mankind; that as there is a great diverſity of theſe obſervable among them, ſo the ſame talents are poſſeſſed in very different proportions by different per-ſons. This variety both in the kind and

degree

degree of mental accomplishments, while it indicates that man was formed for society, doth likewise clearly point out the respective stations in life which every individual is best calculated to fill and to adorn. Education, as it is well or ill directed, may invigorate or weaken the natural powers of the mind, but it cannot produce or annihilate them.

How much soever these powers may be perverted or misapplied, by the folly and ignorance of men, it cannot be denied, that the variety with which they are bestowed, is both a wise and beneficent contrivance of the Author of nature; since a diversity and a subordination of intellectual accomplishments are no less necessary to the order and good government of society, than a subordination of rank and fortune. By these means the general business of life is most successfully carried on; men become mutually dependent upon, and subservient to, the necessities of each other: some apply themselves to agriculture and commerce; while

while others, of a more contemplative difpofition, or of a more lively imagination, de-
dicate their time to philofophy and the liberal arts.

Of thofe who have applied themfelves to
the cultivation of either, a fmall number
only are qualified to extend their empire,
and advance their improvement in any confiderable degree. To explore unbeaten tracks,
and make new difcoveries in the regions of
Science; to invent the defigns, and perfect
the productions of Art, is the province of
Genius alone. Thefe ends are the objects to
which it conftantly afpires; and the attainment of thefe ends can only fall within the
compafs of the few enlightened, penetrating,
and capacious minds, that feem deftined by
Providence for enlarging the fphere of human knowledge and human happinefs. The
bulk of the literary part of mankind muft
be contented to follow the path marked out
by fuch illuftrious leaders.

Having

Having fuggefted the objects to which
Genius naturally afpires, it will be more
eafy to difcover the means by which it attains them; or, in other words, the principal ingredients which conftitute this fingular accomplifhment. Thefe are IMAGI-
NATION, JUDGMENT, and TASTE. We fhall
confider therefore the peculiar nature of thefe
different qualities, and point out the particular efficacy of each, and the combined effects of all, in accomplifhing the purpofes
of Genius.

That Imagination is the quality of all
others moft effentially requifite to the exiftence of Genius, will univerfally be acknowledged.

Imagination is that faculty whereby the
mind not only reflects on its own operations, but which affembles the various ideas
conveyed to the underftanding by the canal
of fenfation, and treafured up in the repo-
fitory of the memory, compounding or disjoining

joining them at pleasure; and which, by its plaftic power of inventing new affociations of ideas, and of combining them with infinite variety, is enabled to prefent a creation of its own, and to exhibit fcenes and objects which never exifted in nature. So indifpenfibly neceffary is this faculty in the compofition of Genius, that all the difcoveries in fcience, and all the inventions and improvements in art, if we except fuch as have arifen from mere accident, derive their origin from its vigorous exertion *. At the fame time it muft be confeffed, that all the falfe and fallacious fyftems of the former, and all the irregular and illegitimate performances in the latter, which have ever

---

* It would be talking with great impropriety, to afcribe either the one or the other to the force of an acute and penetrating Judgment; fince it is the chief province of this faculty, as will immediately be fhewn, to employ its difcerning power in demonftrating, by juft reafoning and induction, the truth and importance of thofe difcoveries, and the utility of thofe inventions; while the inventions and difcoveries themfelves muft be effectuated by the power of a plaftic or warm imagination.

been

been obtruded upon mankind, may be juftly imputed to the unbounded extravagance of the fame faculty : fuch effects are the natural confequences of an exuberant imagination, without any proportionable fhare of the reafoning talent. It is evidently neceffary therefore, in order to render the productions of Genius regular and juft, as well as elegant and ingenious, that the difcerning and coercive power of judgment fhould mark and reftrain the excurfions of a wanton imagination; in other words, that the aufterity of reafon fhould blend itfelf with the gaiety of the graces. Here then we have another ingredient of Genius; an ingredient effential to its conftitution, and without which it cannot poffibly be exhibited to full advantage, even an accurate and penetrating JUDGMENT.

The proper office of JUDGMENT in compofition, is to compare the ideas which imagination collects; to obferve their agreement or difagreement, their relations and refemblances;

blances; to point out fuch as are of a homogeneous nature; to mark and reject fuch
as are difcordant; and finally, to determine
the truth and utility of the inventions or difcoveries which are produced by the power of
imagination †. This faculty is, in all its
operations, cool, attentive, and confiderate.
It canvaffes the defign, ponders the fentiments, examines their propriety and connection, and reviews the whole compofition
with fevere impartiality. Thus it appears to
be in every refpect a proper counterbalance
to the RAMBLING and VOLATILE power of
IMAGINATION. The one, perpetually attempting to foar, is apt to deviate into the
mazes of error; while the other arrefts the
wanderer in its vagrant courfe, and compels

---

† QUINTILIAN, who poffeffed all the ingredients
of Genius in a high and almoft equal degree, feems to
confider Judgment as fo effential a one in its compofition, that he will not allow the name of *Invention* to
any difcovery of imagination which has not paffed the
teft of reafon : *Nec inveniffe quidem credo eum qui non
judicavit.*

it

it to follow the path of nature and of truth.

Indeed the principal ufe and the proper fphere of judgment, in works of Genius and Art, is to guard an author or an artift againft the faults he may be apt to commit, either in the defign or execution of his work, rather than to affift him in the attainment of any uncommon beauty, a tafk which this faculty is by no means qualified to accomplifh. We may alfo obferve, that it is chiefly employed in pointing out the moft obvious blemifhes in any performance, and efpecially fuch as are contrary to the rules of art. There are other blemifhes, perhaps no lefs confiderable, that utterly efcape its notice; as there are certain peculiar and delicate beauties of which it can take no cognifance. Both thefe are the objects of that faculty which we diftinguifhed by the name of TASTE, and confidered as the laft ingredient in the compofition of Genius.

We

" We may define TASTE to be that internal fenfe, which, by its own exquifitely nice fenfibility, without the affiftance of the reafoning faculty, diftinguifhes and determines the various qualities of the object fubmitted to its cognifance; pronouncing, by its own arbitrary verdict, that they are grand or mean, beautiful or ugly, decent or ridiculous *." From this definition it appears, that Tafte is defigned as a fupplement to the defects of the power of judgment, at leaft in canvaffing the merit of the performances of art. Thefe indeed are the fubjects on which it exercifes its difcerning talent with the greateft propriety, as well as with the greateft probability of fuccefs: its dominion, however, is in fome degree univerfal, both in the Arts and Sciences; though that dominion is much more abfolute, and more legitimate in the former than it is in the

---

* Omnes enim, tacito quodam fenfu, fine ulla arte aut ratione, quæ fint in artibus ac rationibus recta ac prava dijudicant. CICERO de Orat. lib. iii, cap. 50.

latter.

latter.  The truth is, to bring philofophical
fubjects to the tribunal of Tafte, or to employ this faculty principally in their examination, is extremely dangerous, and naturally productive of abfurdity and error.
The order of things is thereby reverfed;
reafon is dethroned, and fenfe ufurps the
place of judgment.  Tafte therefore muft be
contented to act an inferior and fubordinate
part in the refearches of fcience : it muft not
pretend to take the lead of reafon, but hum-
bly follow the path marked out by it.  In
the defigns and works of art, the cafe is
quite otherwife.  Inftead of being directed
by judgment, it claims the direction in its
turn; its authority is uncontrolable, and
there lies no appeal from its decifions.  Indeed it is well qualified to decide with precifion and certainty on fubjects of this kind;
for it poffeffes a perfpicacity of difcernment
with regard to them, which reafon can by no
means pretend to, even on thofe fubjects that
are the moft adapted to its nature.  So much
more perfect are the fenfes than the underftanding.

ftanding. We fhall illuftrate thefe remarks
by an example.

Let us fuppofe two perfons, the one pos-
feffed of a comprehenfive and penetrating
judgment, without any refinement or deli-
cacy of tafte; the other endued with the
moft exquifite fenfibility of tafte, without
any extraordinary proportion of the reafoning talent, both fet to work in examining
the merit of fome mafterly production of
art, that admired piece of hiftory-painting,
for inftance, of the Crucifixion, by MICHAEL
ANGELO, and obferve their different procedure, and the very different remarks they
will make. The former meafures with his
eye the exact proportion of every figure in
the piece; he confiders how far the rules of
art are obferved in the defign and ordonnance; whether the group of fubordinate
figures naturally lead the eye to the capital
one, and fix the attention principally upon
it; and whether the artift has given a proper variety of expreffion to the countenances
of

of the feveral fpectators. Upon difcovering
that the painter had exactly conformed to
the rules of his art in all thefe particulars,
he would not only applaud his judgment,
but would alfo give teftimony to his maftery and fkill; without, however, having any
true feeling of thofe uncommon beauties
which conftitute real merit in the art of
painting. Such would be the procedure and
remarks of the man of mere judgment.
Confider now, on the other hand, in what a
different manner the man of tafte will proceed, and in what manner he will be affected. Inftead of attending, in the firft place,
to the juft proportions of the various figures
exhibited in the draught, however neceffary
to be obferved; inftead of remarking, with
approbation, the judgment and ingenuity
difplayed by the artift in the uniformity of
defign, and in the regularity and juftnefs
that appear in the difpofition of the feveral
figures of the piece; he fixes his eye upon
the principal one, in which he obferves the
various contorfions of the counfenance, the
natural

natural expreffions of agonifing pain, mixed
however with an air of divine benignity
and compaffion. Then he paffes on to the
contemplation of the inferior and fubordinate figures, in which he perceives a variety of oppofite paffions, of rage and terror,
of admiration and pity, ftrongly marked in
their different countenances; and feels the
correfponding emotions in their utmoft
ftrength which thofe feveral paffions are
calculated to infpire. In a word, the man
of judgment approves of and admires what
is merely mechanical in the piece; the man
of tafte is ftruck with what could only be
effected by the power of Genius. Where-
ever nature is juftly reprefented, wherever
the features of any one paffion are forcibly
expreffed, to thofe features his attention is
attracted, and he dwells on the contemplation of them with intenfe and exquifite
pleafure. The fenfations of the former are
cool, weak, and unaffecting throughout;
thofe of the latter are warm, vivid, and
deeply interefting; or, to fpeak more properly,

perly, the one reafons, the other feels †. But as no reafoning can enable a man to form an idea of what is really an object of fenfation, the moft penetrating judgment can never fupply the want of an exquifite fenfibility of tafte. In order therefore to re- lifh and to judge of the productions of Ge- nius and of Art, there muft be an internal perceptive power, exquifitely fenfible to all the impreffions which fuch productions are ca- pable of making on a fufceptible mind.

This internal power of perception, which we diftinguifh by the name of TASTE, and which we have fhewn to be fo neceffary for enabling us to judge properly concerning works of imagination, does not appear to be requifite, in the fame degree, in the refearches of Science. In this department, reafon reaffumes the reins, points out and prefcribes

---

† Non ratione aliqua, fed motu nefcio an inenarra- bili judicatur. Neque hoc ab ullo fatis explicari puto, licet multi tentaverint. QUINT. *Inſtit.* lib. vi.

the

the flight of fancy, affigns the office, and determines the authority of tafte, which, as we have already obferved, muft here be contented to act a fecondary part. In philofophical fpeculations a conftant appeal is made to the faculty of Reafon, not to that of Imagination; principles are laid down, arguments are adduced, phenomena are explained, and their confequences inveftigated. Hence it follows, that in the whole procefs judgment is much more exercifed than tafte. Yet fome fcope is alfo afforded for the exercife of the latter faculty; for as all difcoveries in fcience are the work of imagination, which will be afterwards particularly fhewn; fo tafte may be very properly exerted in the illuftration of thofe difcoveries which have obtained the fanction of reafon; provided that, in this cafe, tafte and imagination act under the direction, and fubmit to the controling power of judgment.

On the other hand, judgment has a particular province affigned to it, in examining

C the

the works of Genius and Art; though, with regard to thefe, it acts an inferior part, as tafte does in the former cafe. Judgment muft not prefume to take cognifance of thofe exquifite and delicate beauties, which are properly the objects of the laft mention-ed faculty; but it may determine concerning regularity, juftnefs, and uniformity of de-fign, and concerning propriety of fentiment and expreffion. All thefe fall within its fphere; and its decifions in thefe refpects command our affent.

Upon the whole; as JUDGMENT and TASTE may be alternately exercifed in the fphere of each other, and ought to act with combined influence, though with different power, and with different degrees of exertion; fo both thefe faculties muft be united with a high degree of imagination, in order to conftitute improved and confummate Genius.

From the obfervations that have been made on thofe diftinguifhing faculties of the human mind,

mind, IMAGINATION, JUDGMENT, and
TASTE, it is evident, that not any one of thefe
talents, in whatever degree we may fuppofe
it to exift, can of itfelf attain the objects of
Genius. Even imagination, the moft effential and predominant ingredient in the
compofition of this character, if we fuppofe it to exift in a man without any confiderable proportion of the other faculties,
will be miferably inadequate to the objects
juft mentioned; for though it may, by its
own native vigour, fometimes ftrike out an
important difcovery, either in fcience or in
art, yet this will no way avail, if there is
not a fufficient ftrength of reafon beftowed
to prove its truth and utility. Such a difcovery will often, however undefervedly, expofe the author to ridicule; and the utmoft
reward he can hope for of his labour, is to
gain the character of a romantic vifionary,
or an adventurous, but vain, projector;
though the fame difcovery more clearly re-
vealed, and more fully demonftrated, by another perfon, poffeffed perhaps of no higher

degree

degree of imagination, but endued with a
more penetrating judgment, will procure
him that reputation and honour, of which
the greateſt part was due to the firſt author.

Having conſidered the nature of the different faculties of IMAGINATION, JUDGMENT
and TASTE, and pointed out their reſpective
exertions; having alſo ſhewn that imagination, the moſt diſtinguiſhing of theſe faculties,
is of itſelf inſufficient to attain the objects of
Genius; we ſhall now take a view of Imagination, Judgment, and Taſte, as forming
by their union the full perfection of Genius,
and ſhall obſerve their combined effects in
compoſition.

If we ſuppoſe a PLASTIC and COMPREHEN-
SIVE IMAGINATION, an ACUTE INTELLECT,
and an exquiſite SENSIBILITY and REFINE-
MENT of TASTE, to be all combined in one perſon, and employed in the arts or ſciences, we
may eaſily conceive, that the effect of ſuch an
union

union will be very extraordinary. In such a case, these faculties going hand in hand together, mutually enlighten and assist each other. Imagination takes a long and adventurous, but secure flight, under the guiding rein of judgment; which, though naturally cool and deliberate, catches somewhat of the ardor of the former in its rapid course. To drop the allusion, imagination imparts vivacity to judgment, and receives from it solidity and justness : TASTE bestows ELEGANCE on both, and derives from them PRECISION and SENSIBILITY. The effect of the union of these qualities in composition, will be observed and felt by every reader. It will appear in new and surprising sentiments, in splendid imagery, in just and nervous reasoning, and in eloquent, graceful, and animated expression. Hence, in the writings of an author who possesses the qualities above mentioned in a high degree, we are convinced, pleased, or affected, according to the various strain of his composition, as it is adapted to the

under-

underſtanding, the imagination, or the
heart.

We ſhall not pretend to aſcertain the
exact proportion of the ſeveral ingredients
which enter into the formation of Genius;
it is ſufficient to have ſhewn, that they muſt
all ſubſiſt in a conſiderable degree, a truth
which we have deduced from the objects of
Genius themſelves. We ſhall only remark,
that as among the faculties of which Genius is compoſed, imagination bears the
principal and moſt diſtinguiſhing part, ſo of
courſe it will and ought to be the predominant one. An exact equilibrium of the reaſoning and inventive powers of the mind,
is perhaps utterly incompatible with their
very different natures; but though a perfect
equipoiſe cannot ſubſiſt, yet they may be
diſtributed in ſuch a proportion, as to pre-
ſerve nearly an equality of weight; and,
notwithſtanding the opinion which is generally and abſurdly entertained to the contrary, the powers of imagination and rea-

ſon

ſon may be united in a very high degree, though this is not always the caſe, in the ſame perſon.

Should any one be inclined to controvert the account we have given of the nature and ingredients of Genius, and, inſtead of allowing it to be a compound quality, be of opinion that it is conſtituted and charac- teriſed by Imagination alone; or, in other words, that Genius and Imagination are one and the ſame thing; we ſhall not diſ- pute with him about words; for the ingre- dients of Genius depend intirely upon the acceptation in which we take it, and upon the extent and offices we aſſign to it. It is evident, from the idea we have given of its objeꜩs, that the ingredients above enume- rated and explained, are neceſſary to the at- tainment of them; and therefore we admit thoſe ingredients into its compoſition. If, after all, any perſon ſhould ſtill continue to think that Genius and Imagination are ſyn- onymous terms, and that the powers of the

C 4                                former

former are moſt properly expreſſed by thoſe of the latter; let him reflect, that if the former is characteriſed by fancy alone, without any proportion of judgment, there is ſcarce any means left us of diſtinguiſhing betwixt the flights of Genius and the reveries of a Lunatic.

It is likewiſe to be obſerved, that we regard the *Iliad* and the *Odyſſey* as works of Genius, not only becauſe there appears an aſtoniſhing diſplay of Imagination in the invention of characters and incidents in thoſe admired productions; but alſo, becauſe that Imagination is regulated by the niceſt judgment; becauſe the characters are juſtly drawn, as well as uniformly ſupported; and the incidents as judiciouſly diſpoſed, as they are happily invented: and, laſtly, becauſe regularity and beauty of deſign, as well as maſtery of execution, are conſpicuous throughout the whole. Take away the excellencies now mentioned, and you deprive thoſe divine poems of half their merit:

merit : deftitute of thefe excellencies, they could only be confidered as the rapfodies of an extravagant and lawlefs fancy, not as the productions of well regulated and confummate Genius.

From all that has been faid, one obvious remark naturally arifes, that induftry and application, though they may improve the powers of Genius, can never fuperfede the neceffity, or fupply the want of them. The truth of this obfervation is abundantly confirmed by the different ftrain and fuccefs of the writings of different authors; which writings ferve to fhew, that as Genius is the vital principle which animates every fpecies of compofition, the moft elaborate performances without it, are no other than a lifelefs mafs of matter, frigid and uninterefting, equally deftitute of paffion, fentiment and fpirit. To conclude : A performance void of Genius, is like an opake body viewed in a dark and cloudy day; but a performance

ance irradiated with the beams of this divine quality, is like an object rendered pellucid and tranſparent by the ſplendor of the ſun.

SECTION

# SECTION II.

### OF THE

## USUAL INDICATIONS

### OF

# GENIUS.

HAVING endeavoured, in the preceding section, to explain the nature, and determine the ingredients of Genius; and having likewise pointed out the effects of those ingredients in composition, we shall now proceed to consider the most usual indications of the above mentioned quality.

It may be observed in general, that Genius is neither uniform in the manner, nor periodical with regard to the time of its appearance. The manner depends upon the original constitution and peculiar modifica-

tion

tion of the mental powers, together with
the correfponding organifation of the corpo-
real ones, and upon that mutual influence
of both, in confequence of which the mind
receives a particular bias to one certain object, and acquires a talent for one art or
fcience rather than another.   The period
depends fometimes upon a fortunate accident
encouraging its exertion, fometimes upon a
variety of concurring caufes ftimulating its
ardor, and fometimes upon that natural ef-
fervefcence of mind (if we may thus exprefs
it) by which it burfts forth with irrefiftible
energy, at different ages, in different perfons, not only without any foreign aid, but
in oppofition to every obftacle that arifes in
its way.

With regard to the firft of thefe points :
though Genius difcovers itfelf in a vaft variety of forms, we have already obferved,
that thofe forms are diftinguifhed and characterifed by one quality common to them
all, poffeffed indeed in very different degrees,
                                                and

and exerted in very different capacities; this
quality, it will be underſtood, is Imagination. The mental powers unfold themſelves
in exact proportion to our neceſſities and
occaſions for exerciſing them. Imagination
therefore being that faculty which lays the
foundation of all our knowledge, by collecting and treaſuring up in the repoſitory of
the memory thoſe materials on which Judgment is afterwards to work, and being peculiarly adapted to the gay, delightful, vacant ſeaſon of childhood and youth, appears
in thoſe early periods in all its puerile bril-
liance and ſimplicity, long before the reaſoning faculty diſcovers itſelf in any conſiderable degree. Imagination however, in
general, exerciſes itſelf for ſome time indiſ-
criminately on the various objects preſented
to it by the ſenſes, without taking any particular or determinate direction ; and ſometimes the peculiar bent and conformation of
Genius is diſcernible only in the advanced
period of youth. The mind, as ſoon as it
becomes capable of attending to the repreſentation

fentation it receives of outward objects by the miniftry of the fenfes, views fuch a reprefentation with the curiofity of a ftranger, who is prefented with the profpect of an agreeable and uncommon fcene. The novelty of the objects at firft only affects it with pleafure and furprife. It afterwards furveys, revolves, and reviews them fucceffively one after another; and, at laft, after having been long converfant with them, felects one diftinguifhed and favourite object from the reft, which it purfues with its whole bent and vigour. There are fome perfons, it is true, in whom a certain bias or talent for one particular art or fcience, rather than another, appears in very early life; and in fo great a degree as would incline us to imagine, that fuch a difpofition and talent muft have been congenial and innate. While perfons are yet children, we difcover in their infantile purfuits the opening buds of Genius; we difcern the rudiments of the Philofopher, the Poet, the Painter, and the Architect.

The

The productions indeed of youthful geniufes will be naturally marked with thofe
improprieties and defects, both in defign,
fentiment and expreffion, which refult from
the florid, exuberant, and undifciplined imagination, that is peculiar to an age wherein
Judgment hath not yet exerted its chaften-
ing power. When the cafe is otherwife,
and this faculty hath attained confiderable
maturity in early youth, it affords no favourable prefage of future grandeur and extent of Genius; for we rarely find fruit on
the tree which puts forth its leaves and
bloffoms on the firft return of fpring *.

Nature

---

* QUINTILIAN confiders thefe forward geniufes as
hafty and untimely growths, like thofe ears of corn,
which fuddenly fpring up in a fhallow foil, without
ftriking their roots deep into the earth, and acquire
the colour, but not the fubftance of full and ripe
grain, before the natural time.

Illud ingeniorum velut præcox genus, non temere unquam pervenit ad frugem. Hi funt qui parva facile fa-
ciunt; & audacia provecti, quicquid illic poffunt, ftatim
oftendunt. Poffunt autem id demum quod in proximo
eft:

Nature requires time to mature her productions; the powers of the mind and body
grow up together, and both acquire their
proper confiftence and vigour by juft degrees; this at leaft is the ordinary courfe
of nature, from which there are few ex-
ceptions.

But though Genius cannot be faid to attain its full perfection till the reafoning faculty, one of its effential ingredients, acquires its utmoft extent and improvement;
yet there are certain indications of its exiftence and powers, even in early life, which
an attentive obferver may eafily difcover,
and which are as various as the forms
wherein it appears.

---

eft: verba continuant; hæc vultu interrito, nulla tar-
dati verecundia proferunt: non multum præftant, fed
cito; non fubeft vera vis, nec penitus immiffis radici-
bus nititur: ut quæ fummo folo fparfa funt femina,
celerius fe effundunt & imitatæ fpicas herbulæ inani-
bus ariftis ante meffem flavefcunt. Quint. *Inftit.*
lib. i. cap. 3.

We

We fhall confider the moft diftinguifhing of thefe forms, and the peculiar indications which charaéterife them. Let us firft obferve the effential indications of philofophic Genius.

Imagination receives a very different modification or form in the mind of a Philofopher, from what it takes in that of a Poet. In the one it extends to all the poffible relations of things; in the other it admits only thofe that are probable, in order to determine fuch as are real. Hence it fhould feem, that in the firft inftance it ought to poffefs greater compafs, and in the laft, greater accuracy. Here then we have one charaéteriftical indication of a Genius for philofophical Science; and that is, accuracy of imagination. Its affociations of ideas will be perfeétly juft and exaét, no extraneous ones will be admitted; it will affemble all that are neceffary to a diftinét conception and illuftration of the fubjeét it contemplates, and difcard fuch as are no way conducive

D                    ducive

ducive to thofe purpofes. This precifion and accuracy in felecting and combining its ideas, appears to proceed from a native regularity, clearnefs, and even ftrength of Imagination, united with a certain *acumen ingenii*, a fharpnefs of difcernment, the true criterions of philofophic Genius.

We may farther obferve, that though Reafon, by flow and gradual fteps attains its utmoft extent of comprehenfion, yet being a very diftinguifhing faculty in the mind of the Philofopher, it appears to advance fafter to maturity in him than in any other perfon; and fome prefages of the future extent of his underftanding may be derived from his firft argumentative effays. He will likewife difcover an acutenefs of perception, a fhrewdnefs and fagacity in his obfervations, remarkable for his years; and will begin early to inftitute comparifons, to connect his ideas, and to judge of the relations in which he ftands to the perfons and objects with which he is furrounded.
This

This seems to be the natural progrefs, and firft exertion of Reafon, in ufeful Science.

Let it be remarked in the laft place, that philofophical Genius is peculiarly diftin-guifhed by a certain moral and contempla-tive turn of mind. It feels a powerful ten-dency to fpeculation, and derives its chief pleafure from it. Not fatisfied with explor-ing the phenomena of nature, it delights to inveftigate their unknown caufes. Such are the ufual indications of philofophic Genius. We fhall next confider the moft remarkable indications of this character in Poetry.

As Imagination is the predominant in-gredient in the compofition of poetic Ge-nius, it will there difcover itfelf in its utmoft exuberance and fecundity. This faculty will naturally difplay its creative power on thofe fubjects which afford fulleft fcope for its exercife; for which reafon it will run into the more pleafing fpecies of fiction, and

will

will be particularly diftinguifhed by a happy
fertility of invention. But though fable
be the ftrain of compofition of all others
moft fuitable and appropriated to the higheft
clafs of poetic Genius, neither its choice
nor its abilities are reftricted to this alone.
It freely indulges itfelf on a variety of fubjects; in the felection of which a Poet is
in a great meafure influenced by his age,
temper, and ruling paffion. Thus poems
defcribing the beauties of nature, the tender tranfports of love, the flattering pro-
fpects of ambition, the affectionate and ardent reciprocations of friendfhip, and the
peaceful pleafures of rural tranquillity, are
often among the firft effays of a young
Bard. We purpofely avoid being fo particular on this branch of our fubject, as we
would otherwife choofe to be, left we fhould
anticipate fome of the obfervations that will
be made on the diftinguifhing characters
of original poetic Genius, in another part
of our Effay.

It

It may not however be improper farther to obferve in this place, that one who is born with a Genius for Poetry, will difco- ver a peculiar relifh and love for it in his earlieft years; and that he will be naturally led to imitate the productions he admires. Imagination, which in every man difplays itfelf before any of the other faculties, will be difcernible in him in a ftate of childhood, and will ftrongly prompt him to Poetry: TASSO, wc arc told, compofed poems when he was only five years of age; POPE, we know, wrote fome accurate little pieces, when he was fcarce twelve; and he him- felf acquaints us, by a beautiful, but doubt- lefs figurative expreffion, that he began to write almoft as foon as he began to fpeak:

As yet a child, nor yet a fool to fame,
I lifp'd in numbers, for the numbers came.

MILTON dedicated his Genius to the Mufes in his earlieft youth: he has prefented us with a few poems written in his thirteenth or fourteenth year, inaccurate indeed, as

was

was natural at fuch an age, efpecially in
one who was afterwards to become fo great
a Poet, but full of the ardor and infpiration
of genuine Poetry. Indeed moft of his ju-
venile pieces, which are very unequal in
their merit, afford the happieft prefages of
that amazing grandeur and extent of Imagination, of which he long after exhibited fo glorious a monument in his *Paradife Loft.*

We fhall only add, that the performances
of a youthful Poet, poffeffed of true Genius,
will always abound with that luxuriance of
imagination, and with that vivacity and
fpirit which are fuitable to his years; but
at the fame time they will generally be deftitute of that chaftity and mafculine vigour
of expreffion, as well as juftnefs and propriety of fentiment, which are only compa-
tible with maturer age †.

The

† That great Mafter of Reafon and Eloquence,
whom we laft quoted, and whom we fhall have frequent

The same VIVACITY and ARDOR of Imagination which indicates the Poet, characterises

---

quent occasion to quote in the course of this Essay, since his sentiments on the subjects of which he treats, are as just as they are elegantly and happily expressed, observes, that luxuriance of Imagination is to be regarded as a favourable indication of future fertility and copiousness of Genius ; advises that it should by all means be encouraged ; and suggests the proper method of encouraging it, without apprehending any danger from its excess.

Nec unquam me in his discentis annis offendat si quid superfuerit. Quin ipsis doctoribus hoc esse curæ velim, ut teneras adhuc mentes more nutricum mollius alant, & satiari velut quodam jucundioris disciplinæ lacte patiantur. Erit illud plenius interim corpus, quod mox adulta ætas astringat. Hinc spes roboris. Maciem namque & infirmitatem in posterum minari solet protinus omnibus membris expressus infans. Audeat hæc ætas plura, & inveniat, & inventis gaudeat, sint licet illa non satis interim sicca & severa. Facile est remedium ubertatis, sterilia nullo labore vincuntur. Illa mihi in pueris natura minimum spei dabit, in qua ingenium judicio præsumitur. Materiam esse primam volo vel abundantiorem, atque ultra quam oporteat fusam. Multum inde decoquent anni, multum ratio limabit, aliquid velut usu ipso deteretur, sit modo unde

excidi

terifes likewife and diftinguifhes the Painter;
the figns only being different by which it is
expreffed. The former endeavours to impart his fentiments and ideas to us by verbal
defcription; the latter fets before our eyes a
ftriking refemblance of the objects of which
he intends to convey an idea, by the ingenious contrivance of various colours deli-
cately blended, and by the proper union of
light and fhade. In order to effect his purpofe, he muft have his imagination poffeffed
with very vivid conceptions of the objects he

---

excidi poffit & quod exculpi. Erit autem, fi non ab
initio tenuem nimium laminam duxerimus, & quam
cælatura altior rumpat. QUINTIL. *Infit.* lib. ii. cap. 4.

CICERO's fentiments on this fubject coincide exactly
with thofe of QUINTILIAN quoted above :

Volo enim, fe efferat in adolefcente fœcunditas : nam
facilius, ficut in vitibus revocantur ea, quæ fefe nimium
profuderunt, quam, fi nihil valet materies, nova far-
menta cultura excitantur: ita volo effe in adolefcente
unde aliquid amputem. Non enim poteft in eo effe
fuccus diuturnus, quod nimis celeriter eft maturitatem
affecutum. *De Orat.* lib. ii. cap. 21.

would

would thus exhibit; otherwise it is impossible he should delineate the transcript of them upon canvas. The Imagination must guide the hand in the design and execution of the whole. A Painter therefore of true Genius, having his fancy strongly impressed and wholly occupied by the most lively conceptions of the objects of which he intends to express the resemblance, has immediate recourse to his pencil, and attempts, by the dexterous use of colours, to sketch out those perfect and living figures which exist in his own mind. He will be frequently observed to employ his talents in this manner; and the eminence and extent of his Genius is indicated by the degree of his success.

Imagination, in a considerable degree, is also requisite to the Musician, who would become excellent in his profession. He must be thoroughly acquainted with the power of sounds in all their variety of combination. His imagination must assist him

in

in combining founds, in order to conftitute
different fpecies of harmony; and his experience of the effects of various modulations,
firft on the ear, and, by the inftrumentality
of this organ on the paffions, muft aid his
fancy in fetting his compofitions to the notes
of mufic. By fuch exercifes a mufical Genius is indicated.

A Talent or Genius for Architecture is
difcovered by a proper union of Imagination and Tafte, directed to the accomplifhment of the ends of this art. The degree
of Imagination neceffary to a maftery in Architecture, depends upon the bounds we affign to it, and the improvements we fuppofe practicable in it. Human ingenuity
hath as yet difcovered only five orders in
this art, which contain all the various
forms of grandeur and beauty, confiftent
with regularity, that have ever been invented; and our modern artifts have confined their ambition to the ftudy and imitation of thofe illuftrious monuments of
Genius

Genius left them by their predeceffors, as
if it were impoffible to invent any other
fuperior or equal models.   To invent
new models of Architecture, would, we
confefs, require great compafs of Imagination.   In fuch inventions however true
Genius delights, and by fuch it is indicated in a very high degree.   To unite in
one confummate plan the various orders
of ancient Architecture, requires indeed a
confiderable fhare of Imagination; but it
may be obferved, that a refined and well
formed Tafte is the principal requifite in
a modern Architect; for though Fancy
may be employed in combining the different orders of Architecture in one general defign, it is the province of Tafte
alone to review the parts thus combined,
and to determine the beauty and gracefulnefs of the whole.   Setting afide, therefore, new inventions in this art, which
can only be effected by an uncommon extent of Imagination, we may venture to
affirm, that the employment of Fancy
and

and Tafte, in the manner above mentioned, is a proper indication of a Genius for Architecture, as well as neces-
fary to the accomplifhment of fuch a Genius.

With refpect to a Genius for Eloquence,
its characteriftical indications are effentially the fame with thofe which denote a
talent for Poetry *. The fame creative
power, the fame extent and force, the
fame impetuofity, and fire of Imagination,
diftinguifh both almoft in an equal degree; with this difference only, that the
latter is permitted to range with a LOOSER
rein than is indulged to the former, which,

---

* Eft enim finitimus Oratori Poeta, numeris adftric-
tior paulo, verborum autem licentia liberior, multis
vero ornandi generibus focius ac pene par; in hoc quidem certe prope idem, nullis ut terminis circumfcribat,
aut definiat jus fuum, quo minus ei liceat eadem illa
facultate, & copia, vagari qua velit. CICERO de Orat.
lib. i. cap. 16.

though

though it may dare to emulate the boldnefs and fublimity of poetic infpiration, is
not allowed to SPORT and WANTON with
fuch WILDNESS and LUXURIANCE.

SECTION

# SECTION III.

## OF THE

# CONNECTION

### BETWIXT

# GENIUS,
# WIT,

### AND

# HUMOUR.

GENIUS, WIT, and HUMOUR, have been confidered by many as words of equivalent fignification; and have therefore been often injudicioufly confounded toge-ther. Some do not perceive the difference betwixt them; and others, not attending to it, ufe thefe expreffions alternately and in-difcriminately. There is however a real difference between thefe accomplifhments; and

and as the subject of this Section is neither
incurious nor unimportant, and is, to us at
least, new, we shall endeavour in the progress of it to explain the nature, and to
mark the essential and peculiar characters
of the above-mentioned qualities: we shall
point out their distinguishing difference, and
shew their mutual connection.

The talents we are treating of are all the
offspring of Imagination, of which quality
however they participate in very different
degrees ; as a much greater share of it is
requisite to constitute true Genius, than is
necessary to constitute either of the other
endowments. Our present inquiry obliges
us to anticipate a little what will afterwards be more fully discussed, by remarking, that Genius is characterised by a copious and plastic, as well as a vivid and extensive Imagination ; by which means it
is equally qualified to invent and create,
or to conceive and describe in the most
lively manner the objects it contemplates.

Such

Such is the nature, and such are the essential characters of Genius. On the other hand, Wit and Humour neither invent nor create; they neither possess the vigour, the compass, nor the plastic power of the other quality. Their proper province is to assemble with alertness those sentiments and images, which may excite pleasantry or ridicule. Hence vivacity and quickness of Imagination form their peculiar characters. In fact, the accomplishments of Wit and Humour, which are so much the objects of applause and envy, are derived from this vivacity of Fancy, united with an exquisite sense of Ridicule. As a proof of this, we need only to observe, that they are generally employed in painting the ridiculous in characters and in manners; and those flashes of wit, and strokes of humour, we so much admire, are by no means the effects of a creative Imagination, the distinguishing characteristic of true Genius; but of a quickness and readiness of fancy in assembling such ideas as lie latent in the mind, till the

combining

combining power of affociation, with the affiftance of the retentive faculty, calls them forth, by the fuggeftion of fome diftant, perhaps but correfponding circumftance. This feems to be no improbable theory of Wit and Humour; which, though akin to each other, and produced by the fame caufes, are however diftinct qualities, and may exift feparately.

The former is the moft fhining, the latter the moft pleafing and the moft ufeful quality. Wit difcovers itfelf in fmart repartees, in ingenious conceits, in fanciful allufions, and in brilliant fentiments. Humour, on the other hand, manifefts itfelf in ludicrous reprefentations, in mafterly ftrokes of manners and character, in fhrewd obfervations, and in facetious argumentation and narrative. This quality may be divided into two kinds; into that which is difplayed in the reprefentation of characters, and may be denominated humour of character; and into that which is difplayed in compofition,

and

and may be called humour in writing. The
firſt conſiſts in the art of marking the follies, the foibles, or the oddities of the character exhibited ſo ſtrongly, and expoſing
them in ſuch a ludicrous light, as to excite
pleaſantry and laughter. Sometimes the
character may be ſo amiable, that its little
peculiarities, inſtead of leſſening our eſteem
or affection, increaſe the former, and conciliate the latter; provided however, thoſe
peculiarities are innocent in themſelves, and
indicate or imply genuine excellence. Of
this kind is the character of Sir ROGER DE
COVERLEY, drawn with the moſt exquiſite
humour, and by the happieſt effort of AD-
DISON's delicate pencil.

Humour in WRITING conſiſts either of
random ſtrokes of RIDICULE and FACE-
TIOUSNESS, occaſionally thrown out, as ſubjects of DROLLERY and PLEASANTRY happen
to occur; or of a vein of IRONY and DELI-
CATE SATIRE, purpoſely diſplayed on a
particular ſubject. Perhaps POPE's *Rape of*
*the*

*the Lock* is the moſt refined piece of HUMOUR in this kind, which any age can boaſt. There remains indeed another ſpecies of Wit and Humour (for it participates of, or at leaſt pretends to both) of the loweſt ſort however, but deſerving ſome attention; that which conſiſts of puns, quibbles, and the petulant ſallies of a rambling and un-diſciplined fancy; and which is ſometimes diſplayed in converſation. This ſpecies of it is not only generally oſtentatious, but ſuperficial. It flaſhes for a little while, and then expires. It ruſhes on with precipitation, and, like a ſhallow ſtream, makes a great noiſe; but the rivulet ſoon dries up, and betrays the penuriouſneſs of the ſource from which it flowed. The converſation-wits reſemble thoſe perſons, whoſe ideas paſs through their minds in too quick ſucceſſion to be diſtinct; but who, nevertheleſs, being endued with a natural volubility of expreſſion, acquit them-ſelves to admiration in company; while one is at a loſs to find either ſenſe or gram-mar in their compoſitions. To become a

man

man of true Wit and Humour, it is neceffary
to *think*; a piece of drudgery which the
Gentlemen we are fpeaking of are too lively
to undergo.

But to return: it appears that WIT and
HUMOUR, though nearly ALLIED to true
Genius, being the offspring of the fame parent, are however of a diftinct nature; fince
the former are produced by the efforts of a
RAMBLING and SPORTIVE Fancy, the latter
proceeds from the copious effufions of a
plaftic Imagination.   Hence it will follow,
that every man of GREAT WIT will not be
a GREAT GENIUS, nor will every man of
GREAT GENIUS be a GREAT WIT.   Thefe
qualities do not always exift together.
Thus SWIFT was not a GENIUS, at leaft of
a very EXALTED kind *, in the fenfe in
which

---

* Perhaps fome of the Dean's moft zealous admi-
rers may be offended with a declaration which excludes
his pretenfions to any extraordinary degree of Genius.
                                                    But

which we have confidered it, nor OSSIAN a Wit. To this perhaps it will be replied, that the Mufe of the latter had caught the complexion of his own temper, which was a melancholy one, partly derived from his natural conftitution, and partly occafioned by the misfortunes of his family ; and that his fubjects, being of the mournful kind, could not admit of the fprightly graces of WIT and HUMOUR. But let it be obferved, that

---

But let them reflect on what fuch pretenfions are founded. I can recollect no performance of the Doctor's, which can juftly denominate him a man of great Genius, excepting his *Gulliver* and his *Tale of a Tub*; in which, it muft be confeffed, he hath united both Invention and Humour : and therefore we allow him to have poffeffed a degree of Genius, proportionable to the degree of Invention difcovered in the above mentioned performances. In that kind of wit and humour which he attempted, though not the moft delicate, he unqueftionably excelled all mankind. In the fcale of Genius, however, we muft affign him an inferior ftation ; fince his Mufe fcarce ever rifes to the region of the Sublime, which is the proper fphere of a great Genius ; but, on the contrary, delights to wallow in the offal and naftinefs of a fty or a kennel.

E 3                              the

the melancholy turn of his mind, which ir-
refiftibly determined him to the choice of
mournful fubjects, is a fufficient proof that
thefe were not only moft fuited to his Genius; but that thofe of a folemn, awful,
and pathetic nature, if we include the wild
and picturefque, as fubfervient to the others,
were the only fubjects in which he was qualified to excel. The lighter ornaments of
WIT would have been unfuitable to the
fublimity of his Genius, and the penfive turn
of his mind. We do not intend to infi-
nuate, that Genius and Wit in the higheft
degree are in general incompatible. They
were united in SHAKESPEAR almoft in an
equal meafure; and YOUNG hath given a
fpecimen of the former in his *Night Thoughts,*
and of the latter in his *Univerfal Paffion*; and
in him they were both united together in a
degree of perfection that has not been equaled, fince the era of the great Poet laft mentioned. We only mean to affert, that the
one may exift without the other, which we
think hath been proved in the cafe of Os-

SIAN

SIAN in particular; though we fhall readily allow, that the fimplicity of manners which prevailed in the times of the CALEDONIAN Bard, a fimplicity that was very unfavoura- ble to the difplay of WIT and HUMOUR, joined to the melancholy turn of his own temper, heightened by his afflictions, might have greatly contributed to fupprefs the ta- lents of which we are fpeaking, fuppofing him to have been poffeffed of them. We fhall only add, that there is one cafe in which Wit and Humour may claim the de- nomination of Genius; and that is, when they are accompanied with a rich fund of invention, as in the *Rape of the Lock*; in which, though the machinery of the Sylphs is not the mere creation of the Poet's fancy, yet the particular nature and employment of thofe wonderful aerial beings is altoge- ther his own fiction. In this incomparable heroicomical poem, POPE has inconteftibly eftablifhed his character both as a man of Genius and Wit. It ought however to be remembered, that we allow his title to the

firft

firſt of theſe denominations, not at all upon account of the vein of delicate and refined ſatire which runs through the whole poem, for WIT and HUMOUR could have produced this; but upon account of that ingenious INVENTION, and that PICTURESQUE DE-SCRIPTION, ſo remarkable in it, which thoſe qualities of themſelves could never have produced.

Upon the whole : from the view we have taken of the nature and characters of GE-NIUS, WIT, and HUMOUR, it appears evident, that as theſe qualities are in their nature different from each other, and are marked by certain peculiar and diſtinguiſh-ing characters; ſo they have different ſpheres of exerciſe aſſigned them, in which alone they can diſplay their proper powers to advantage. We may therefore with ſome appearance of reaſon infer, that the connection of the above-mentioned talents is only partial and caſual, not univerſal and neceſ-ſary. This hath in part been already evinced

and

and exemplified by particular inftances; from which it appears, that thofe talents have been fometimes united, and fometimes disjoined in different perfons. As we do not remember to have feen this accidental connection, where a neceffary one at firft view might be expected, accounted for, we fhall conclude the prefent Section with endeavouring to affign the reafons of it.

That Genius, Wit, and Humour, do in common participate of Imagination, we have already acknowledged. This participation indeed forms a NATURAL, but not a NECESSARY connection betwixt thofe qualities. The MODES (if we may fo exprefs it) and DEGREES of this Imagination are fo different, and the tempers of men, on which the exertion of the above mentioned qualities greatly depends, are likewife fo various, that a real union becomes merely FORTUITOUS. In order to make this ftill more evident, as well as farther to account for it, let us recollect the peculiar office of GENIUS,

com-

compared with that of WIT and HUMOUR. The proper office of the former is to INVENT incidents or characters, to CREATE new and uncommon scenery, and to describe every object it contemplates, in the most striking manner, and with the most picturesque circumstances : that of the latter is to represent MEN, MANNERS and THINGS, in such a ludicrous light, as to excite PLEASANTRY, and provoke RISIBILITY. Hence we conclude, that a vigorous, extensive, and PLASTIC Imagination, is the principal qualification of the one, and a quick and lively Fancy the distinguishing characteristic of the other. These qualities do not appear to be connected in any great degree; for what considerable connection is there betwixt a celerity in assembling SIMILAR ideas, together with a lively perception of that SIMILARITY, and the power of inventing a variety of surprising SCENES and INCIDENTS, conceived with the utmost strength and compass of Imagination ? It should even seem that on some occasions an extraordinary
nary

nary vivacity of Fancy, which includes a certain degree of volatility, occafioning the mind to ftart as it were from one object to another, without allowing it time to conceive any of them diftinctly, might be prejudicial to that vivid conception, and that extenfive combination of ideas which indicate and characterife true Genius. In this cafe, the mind, hurried with precipitancy from one theme to another, though it may catch a glimpfe, yet rarely obtains a full view of the object it defires to contemplate. This feems to be the principal reafon why GENIUS, whofe ideas are VIVID and COMPREHENSIVE, is not always united with WIT, whofe conceptions are QUICK and LIVELY, but frequently SUPERFICIAL.

After all, I am fenfible that the pofition laid down above, will to many perfons appear extremely problematical; and that feveral of thofe who can perceive the difference betwixt GENIUS and WIT, will ftill be of opinion, that thefe qualities, however

diftinct

diftinct from each other, are neverthelefs in-
diffolubly connected. After having reflected
a good deal upon the fubject, the fentiments
I have now delivered are the refult of that
reflection ; which fentiments I have endeavoured to confirm by examples, more of
which I could have added, had it appeared
to be neceffary. The truth is, the obferving
that GENIUS and WIT have to all appearance been feparately poffeffed by different
perfons, led me firft to fufpect that their
union was cafual. Proceeding upon this
principle, I have attempted to affign the reafons of it, which I have deduced from the
different natures of thofe qualities themfelves.
Perhaps indeed the examples may appear
more convincing than the arguments. I can
conceive indeed but one other objection to
the former, befides what has been already fuggefted, which is, that men of Genius, confcious of poffeffing fuperior talents, are not
very ambitious of acquiring the reputation
which arifes from WIT. But I cannot think
that this anfwer intirely folves the difficulty,
                                         fup-

suppofing the union of the above-mentioned
qualities really neceffary; for the reputation acquired by the difplay of Wit, however inferior this talent may in fact be, is
often fuperior to that which is acquired by
the difplay of Genius; and we may conclude
in general, that moft of thofe who are poffeffed of it, will be defirous of being diftinguifhed upon that account; and confequently, where it does not difplay itfelf, that it
does not probably in any great degree exift.
It is neceffary to remark, in order to prevent any miftake of my meaning, that while
I endeavoured to prove that Genius and Wit
are not neceffarily connected, I had chiefly
in my eye that fpecies of Wit which is the
fudden effufion of a lively fancy, and which
is poured forth in converfation with a furprifing readinefs and exuberance. That real
Genius frequently exifts without this kind of
it, I am fully convinced by many examples,
which, as the Reader may eafily recollect
them, I fhall not here enumerate. That kind
of Wit and Humour however, which is difcovered

covered in compofition, and which being more the effect of thought, is commonly more juft and folid, though often lefs brilliant, Genius will not fo eafily refign its claim to. Indeed, to declare my own opinion upon a doubtful point, where examples contradict each other, it appears to me moft probable, that true Genius is, we do not fay, univerfally and neceffarily, connected with it; but that it rarely exifts without this kind of Wit; though its exertion may, by various caufes, in a great meafure be fupprefled. When thefe qualities are united together, they mutually affift and improve each other; GENIUS derives VIVACITY from WIT, and WIT derives JUSTNESS and EXTENT of COMPREHENSION from GENIUS.

SECTION

# SECTION IV.

OF THE

## MUTUAL INFLUENCE

OF

## IMAGINATION on TASTE,

AND OF

## TASTE on IMAGINATION;

CONSIDERED AS

INGREDIENTS in the COMPOSITION

OF

# GENIUS.

WE have already confidered IMAGI-
NATION and TASTE as two mate-
rial ingredients in the compofition of GE-
NIUS. The former we have proved to be
the moft effential ingredient, without which
Genius

Genius cannot exift; and that the latter is
indifpenfibly neceffary to render its productions ELEGANT and CORRECT.

We are now to fhew the influence of
thefe qualities on each other, and how they
contribute by their mutual influence to the
improvement and confummation of Genius.
Before we proceed to this difquifition, it
will be proper to recur to the definition of
TASTE, given in a preceding fection, which,
for the fake of precifion, we fhall here re-
peat. "TASTE is that internal fenfe, which,
by its own exquifitely nice perception, without the affiftance of the reafoning faculty,
diftinguifhes and determines the various
qualities of the objects fubmitted to its cognifance, pronouncing them, by its own arbitrary verdict, to be grand or mean, beautiful or ugly, decent or ridiculous." The
fimple principles of Tafte are found in every
man, but the degrees in which they exift,
are as various as can well be imagined: in
fome perfons they are weak and rude; in
others,

others, they are vigorous and refined. The external organs of fenfe, which are the original and fundamental principles of Tafte, are indeed nearly the fame in every one who poffeffes in the moft ordinary degree the effential and conftituent parts of the human frame; but the ideas which are excited in the minds of fome perfons by the influence of outward objects on the fenfes, or by the power of reflection, are very different from thofe excited in the minds of others. Thus two perfons, the one endued with a juft and elegant tafte, the other almoft deftitute of this quality, contemplating a magnificent and well-proportioned building, that of St *Peter's*, for inftance, at *Rome*, will be affected in the moft different manner and degree imaginable. The latter, looking around him with ignorant and infipid curiofity, cafts his eye on the altar and decorations of the church, which captivate his attention, and pleafe his rude fancy, merely by their novelty and fplendor; while he ftares at the magnificence of the

F edifice

edifice with a foolifh face of wonder. The
former, furveying all the fabric together,
is ftruck with admiration of the exact fymmetry, and majeftic grandeur of the whole.
Or if we fhould fuppofe both to be prefented, at the fame time, with the profpect
of a rich, beautiful, and diverfified landfcape, confifting of woods and vallies, of
rocks and mountains, of cafcades and rivers, of groves and gardens, blended together in fweet rural confufion; this inchanting fcene would be contemplated by the
one with indifference, or at leaft with very
little emotion of pleafure, his thoughts being chiefly employed in computing the
produce of fo fertile a fpot; while the
view of fuch a group of delightful objects would throw the other into rapture.
It is natural to afk, whence arifes this
amazing difference in their fenfations? The
outward organ, by which thefe fenfations
are conveyed, is fuppofed to be equally
perfect in both; but the internal feeling
is extremely different. This difference
muft

muft certainly proceed from the transforming power of Imagination, whofe rays illu-
minate the objects we contemplate; and
which, without the luftre fhed on them by
this faculty, would appear unornamented
and undiftinguifhed.

The REFINEMENT and SENSIBILITY of
Tafte likewife, as well as the pleafures it
is calculated to afford, are all derived from
the influence of Imagination over this internal fenfe. By the magical power of
Fancy communicated to it, it is qualified
to difcern the beauties of nature, and the
ingenious productions of art, and to feel
an exquifitely pleafing fenfation from the
furvey of them. Imagination dwells upon
an agreeable object with delight, arrays it
in the moft beautiful colours, and attributes to it a thoufand charms; every repeated view of it increafes thefe charms;
and the Imagination, enraptured with the
contemplation of them, becomes enamoured
of its own creation. Tafte, catching the

con-

contagion from Fancy, contemplates the favourite object with equal tranfport, by which means it acquires and improves its fenfibility : it becomes more fufceptible of pleafure, and more exquifitely acute in its fenfations. Such is the influence of Imagination on Tafte, and fuch are the advantages which the latter derives from the former.

As true Tafte is founded on Imagination, to which it owes all its refinement and elegance; fo a falfe and depraved Tafte is often derived from the fame caufe. Fancy, if not regulated by the dictates of impartial Judgment, is apt to miflead the mind, and to throw glaring colours on objects that poffefs no intrinfic excellence. By this means it happens, that though the principles of a juft Tafte are implanted in the mind of every man of Genius, yet, by a neglect of proper cultivation, or too great an indulgence of the extravagant ramblings of Fancy, thofe

principles

principles are vitiated, and Tafte becomes
fometimes INCORRECT, and fometimes IN-
DELICATE †. The only method left in
fuch a cafe, is to compare the fenfations of
Tafte with the objects that produced them,
and to correct the errors of this fenfe by an
appeal to the dictates of Reafon, in the
points where its authority is legitimate; by
which means Tafte may attain JUSTNESS
and ACCURACY, as by the former exercife
it may acquire SENSIBILITY and REFINE-
MENT, in thofe minds where its principles are implanted in any confiderable degree.

---

† Let it not be imputed to faftidious, much lefs to
malevolent criticifm, if, in order to exemplify the above
remarks, we prefume to obferve, that in a work of real
Genius, and in which the moft fublime fpirit of Poetry
predominates, we mean the *Night Thoughts* of Dr
YOUNG, we meet with feveral inftances of falfe tafte,
in his antithefes and conceits, which, in a great meafure, debafe the grandeur of fome very noble fentiments.

F 3　　　　Having

Having thus pointed out the influence of Imagination on Taſte, let us now conſider the influence of Taſte on Imagination.

As TASTE derives all its SENSIBILITY and REFINEMENT from the prevalence of IMAGINATION, ſo IMAGINATION owes, in a great meaſure, its JUSTNESS and ACCURACY to the CORRECT PRECISION of a well regulated TASTE. The excurſions of Fancy, undirected by Judgment or Taſte, are always extravagant; and if we ſhould ſuppoſe a compoſition to be conceived and executed by the firſt mentioned faculty alone, it would be an unintelligible rhapſody, a mere maſs of confuſion, compounded of a number of heterogeneous and diſcordant parts. Though Imagination has by far the greateſt ſhare of merit in the productions of Genius, yet, in one view, it may be conſidered as acting a ſubordinate part, as exerting its energy under the prudent reſtrictions of Judgment, and the chaſtening animadverſions

fions of Tafte. In fact, the proper office of
Fancy is only to collect the materials of
compofition; but, as a heap of ftones,
thrown together without art or defign, can
never make a regular and well proportioned
building; fo the effufions of Fancy, without
the fuperintending and directing powers
above-mentioned, can never produce a masterly compofition in Science or in Art. Judgment therefore muft arrange in their proper order the materials which Imagination
has collected; and it is the office of Tafte
to beftow thofe diftinguifhing.graces, which
may give DIGNITY and ELEGANCE to the
feveral parts, as well as EXCELLENCE and
ACCURACY to the whole. Such is the province of Tafte, and fuch its INFLUENCE on
works of Imagination.

From the furvey we have taken of the
MUTUAL INFLUENCE of thefe different faculties, it appears, that they are equally indebted to each other; and that if, on the
one hand, Imagination beftows SENSIBILITY

F 4 and

and REFINEMENT on Tafte, fo on the other, Tafte imparts JUSTNESS and PRECISION to Imagination; while Genius is confummated by the proper union of both thefe faculties with that of Judgment, and derives from their combined efficacy all its energy, accuracy, and elegance.

SECTION

# SECTION V.

## OF THE

## DIFFERENT DEGREES

### OF

## G E N I U S,

### AND ITS

## VARIOUS MODES of EXERTION.

GENIUS is a word of extenſive and various ſignification. The ſpheres of its exerciſe, and the degrees of its exertion, are very different.

Some perſons poſſeſs ſuch force and com-paſs of Imagination, as to be able by the power of this faculty to conceive and pre-ſent to their own minds, in one diſtinct view, all the numerous and moſt diſtant re-lations of the objects on which they employ

it ;

it ; by which means they are qualified to make great improvements and difcoveries in the arts and fciences. The mind in this cafe has recourfe to and relies on its own fund. Confcious of its native energy, it delights to expand its faculties by the moft vigorous exertion, Ranging through the unbounded regions of nature and of art, it explores unbeaten tracks of thought, catches a glimpfe of fome objects which lie far beyond the fphere of ordinary obfervation, and obtains a full and diftinct view of others.

We may farther obferve, that Genius may, in a very confiderable though much lefs proportion, be difplayed in the illuftration of thofe truths, or the imitation of thofe models, which it was incapable originally to difcover or invent. To comprehend and explain the one, or to exprefs a juft refemblance of the other, fuppofes and requires no contemptible degree of Genius in the Author or Artift who fucceeds in the attempt.
Thus

Thus we allow MACLAURIN, who has explained the Principles of NEWTON's Philosophy, and STRANGE, who has copied the Cartoons of RAPHAEL, to have been both of them men of Genius in their refpective profeffions, though not men of original Genius; for the former did not poffefs that COMPASS of IMAGINATION, and that DEPTH of DISCERNMENT, which were neceffary to difcover the doctrines of the *Newtonian* Syftem; nor the latter that FERTILITY and FORCE of Imagination, that were requifite to invent the defign, and exprefs the dignity, grace and energy, difplayed in the ORIGINALS of the *Italian* Painter.

A certain degree of Genius is likewife manifefted in the more exquifite productions of the mechanical arts. To conftitute an excellent Watchmaker, or even Carpenter, fome fhare of this quality is requifite. In moft of the Arts indeed, of which we are fpeaking, Induftry, it muft be granted, will in a great meafure fupply the place of Genius;

nius; and dexterity of performance may be acquired by habit and sedulous application: yet in others of a more elegant kind, these will by no means altogether supersede its use and exercise; since it can alone bestow those finishing touches that bring credit and reputation to the workman. Every ingenious artist, who would execute his piece with uncommon nicety and neatness, must really work from his imagination. The model of the piece must exist in his own mind. Therefore the more vivid and perfect his ideas are of this, the more exquisite and complete will be the copy.

In some of the mechanical, and in all the liberal Arts, it is not only necessary that artists should possess a certain share of Imagination, in order to attain excellence in their different professions; but that share of which they are possessed, must principally turn upon one particular object. It is this BIAS of the mind to one individual art rather than another, which both indicates and con-

conftitutes what we commonly call a GE-
NIUS for it. This BIAS appears in fome
perfons very early, and very remarkably;
and when it does fo, it ought doubtlefs to
be regarded as the fovereign decree of Nature, marking out the ftation and deftiny of
her children.

It cannot be denied, that a great degree
of Genius is difcovered in the invention of
mechanical arts, efpecially if they are by the
firft efforts advanced to any confiderable
perfection; for invention of every kind is a
fignal proof of Genius. The firft inventer
of a Watch, an Orrery, or even a common
Mill, however fimple it may now appear in
its machinery and ftructure, was unqueftionably a man of an extraordinary mechanical Genius. The improvement of thefe
inventions is likewife a certain criterion of a
Genius for them; the degree of which talent
is always juftly rated in proportion to the
improvements made by it, confidered in connection with the art in which they are made.

We

We ſhall not here inquire into the comparative utility and importance of the feveral Arts, whether liberal or mechanical, in
order to determine the particular degree of
Genius requiſite to an excellence in each of
them. Let it ſuffice to obferve in general,
that as in the former Imagination hath a
wider range, ſo a greater degree of Genius
may be difplayed in thefe than in the other.
Hence we infer their ſuperior dignity, tho'
perhaps not their ſuperior utility. In the
latter indeed, Imagination is very intenfely
exercifed; but it is more confined in its ope-
ration: inſtead of rambling from one theme
to another, it dwells on a ſingle objeɛt, till
it has contemplated it fully and at leifure;
whereas in the others, it forms a leſs particular, but more comprehenfive view of the
objeɛts ſubmitted to its cognifance: it takes
them in at one glance, though it does not
mark their features ſo minutely. A larger
compafs of Imagination therefore is requiſite to conſtitute excellence in the one, and
a greater compreffion of this faculty (if we
may

may ufe the term) to produce eminence in the other.

Genius likewife, when left to follow its own fpontaneous impulfe, appears in a great variety of forms as well as of degrees. Its modes of exertion are very different. Some-times it leads to philofophical fpeculations, and animates the ardor of the Philofopher in his experiments and refearches, in his in-veftigation of caufes and effects, of the order of Providence, and the conftitution of the human mind; and while it points out the objects to which he fhould direct his ftudies, it adapts the mental powers to the purfuit, and qualifies them for the attainment of thofe objects; by communicating that force of imagination, and that depth of difcern-ment which are neceffary to his fuccefs: at other times, indulging its own native bent, it ftrikes out a path for itfelf through the wild romantic regions of Poetry and Fable; and from the infinite variety of ob-jects prefented to it in thofe fields of fiction,

felects

selects such as are most adapted to its nature and powers. Sometimes Genius, still following its own peculiar bias, sketches out, with a happy fertility of invention, the designs of the Painter, and imparts dignity, elegance and expression to the several figures of his piece. Sometimes it appears to great advantage in the graceful elocution, the impetuous ardor, and the impassioned sentiments of the Orator. Sometimes it displays its power in the combination of musical sounds. Sometimes it discovers itself in uniting, by the power of a lively imagination and exquisite taste, the various forms of elegance and magnificence in one consummate model of Architecture. Or, lastly, taking an humbler aim, it sometimes unfolds itself, not indeed with so much power and extent, but still with very considerable energy, in the ingenious inventions and exquisite improvements of the mechanical Arts. So diversified are the forms of Genius, and so various its modes of exertion.

There

There are many indeed, in whom there are no ſtriking ſignatures of this quality diſcernible in any of its forms, who neverthelefs poffefs a confiderable ſhare of that faculty by which it is chiefly conſtituted. Theſe perſons, poffeffing the fundamental qualification of Genius, may, by the force of application, in ſome meaſure ſupply the want of that appropriated Imagination, which confers a talent for one particular art; but can never reach that degree of excellence in their reſpective profeſſions, which a natural impulſe of Genius to its correſponding object, directed with prudence, and aided by proper culture, is calculated to attain. In others, however, the particular indications and EVOLUTIONS of Genius (to uſe a military phraſe) are very remarkable. By attending carefully to theſe SYMPTOMS (if we may alſo adopt a phyſical term) by marking and encouraging their progreſs, Arts and Sciences may be carried to the higheſt degree of perfection, to which human Genius is capable of advancing them.

G           A N

# AN ESSAY ON GENIUS.

## BOOK II.

### OF

## ORIGINAL GENIUS,

### ITS

### INDICATIONS, EXERTION, AND EFFECTS.

# SECTION I.

OF

## THAT DEGREE OF

# G E N I U S,

WHICH IS PROPERLY DENOMINATED

# O R I G I N A L.

WE have in the preceding part of this Essay treated of Genius in general, and have pointed out its objects, ingredients and effects, as well as suggested its various modes of exertion. We shall now proceed a step higher, and consider that degree of Genius, which, upon account of its superior excellence, deserves the name of ORIGINAL. The observations we have hitherto made on Genius indiscriminately, were only intended as an Introduction to the remarks

we

we propofe to make in this book on the
fubject of original Genius ; to explain the
nature, properties, and effects of which, is
the principal defign of this Effay.

It may be proper to obferve, that by the
word ORIGINAL, when applied to Genius,
we mean that NATIVE and RADICAL power
which the mind poffeffes, of difcovering
fomething NEW and UNCOMMON in every
fubject on which it employs its faculties.
This power appears in various forms, and
operates with various energy, according to
its peculiar modification, and the particular
degree in which it is beftowed.   Thus it as-
fumes, as we have feen, a different form,
and appears likewife in a different degree
in the mind of the Philofopher, from what
it doth in that of the Poet or Painter.   It
is not our prefent bufinefs to inquire what
are the proportions and modifications of
fancy neceffary to conftitute a Genius for
particular arts or fciences, as diftinguifhed
from each other, fince this would be an anticipation

ticipation of what is intended to be the fubject of fome following Sections. In this we
confider ORIGINAL GENIUS as a GENERAL
talent, which may be exerted in any profeffion, in order to obferve how happily it is
calculated to attain the objects it has in
view. We fhall only farther previoufly remark, that the word ORIGINAL, confidered
in connection with Genius, indicates the
DEGREE, not the KIND of this accomplifhment, and that it always denotes its higheft
DEGREE.

Philofophers have diftinguifhed two general fources of our ideas, from which we
draw all our knowledge, SENSATION and
REFLECTION. Very different ideas however
are excited in the minds of fome, from thofe
excited in the minds of others, even by the
firft of thefe, which may be faid to be the
original fountain of our knowledge, though
the ideas produced by it are conveyed by
organs common to human nature; and ftill
more different ideas are excited in the minds

of

of different perfons by the other faculty,
that of REFLECTION. Some perfons indeed
have few ideas except fuch as are derived
from fenfation; they feldom ruminate upon,
revolve, and compare the impreffions made
upon their minds, unlefs at the time they
are made, or while they are recent in their
remembrance: hence they become incapable of tracing thofe relations and analogies which exift in nature, but which can
only be traced by men of a comprehenfive
Imagination and penetrating Judgment.
Others, endued with thefe qualities, are
rendered thereby capable of affociating and
disjoining, of comparing and transforming
their ideas in fuch a manner, as to perceive almoft all their poffible relations; by
which means they are qualified to difcover the latent truths of fcience, and to
produce the nobleft monuments of human
ingenuity in the feveral arts. In other
words, they by thefe means become original Geniufes in that particular art or
fcience, to which they have received the

moft

moſt remarkable bias from the hand of
Nature.

ORIGINAL GENIUS is diſtinguiſhed from
every other degree of this quality, by a more
vivid and a more comprehenſive Imagination, which enables it both to take in a
greater number of objeɛts, and to conceive
them more diſtinɛtly; at the ſame time that
it can expreſs its ideas in the ſtrongeſt colours, and repreſent them in the moſt ſtriking light. It is likewiſe diſtinguiſhed by
the ſuperior quickneſs, as well as juſtneſs
and extent, of the aſſociating faculty; ſo
that with ſurpriſing readineſs it combines at
once every homogeneous and correſponding
idea, in ſuch a manner as to preſent a complete portrait of the objeɛt it attempts to deſcribe. But, above all, it is diſtinguiſhed by
an inventive and plaſtic Imagination, by
which it ſketches out a creation of its own,
diſcloſes truths that were formerly unknown,
and exhibits a ſucceſſion of ſcenes and events
which were never before contemplated or
con-

conceived. In a word, it is the peculiar character of original Genius to ftrike out a path for itfelf whatever fphere it attempts to occupy; to ftart new fentiments, and throw out new lights on every fubject it treats. It delights in every fpecies of fiction, and fometimes difcovers itself in the more fevere inveftigations of caufes and effects. It is diftinguifhed by the moft uncommon, as well as the moft furprifing combinations of ideas; by the novelty, and not unfrequently by the fublimity and boldnefs of its imagery in compofition.

Thus much with regard to the nature and characteriftics of original Genius in general. What we are next to confider, is its particular and fingular efficacy in inriching Science with new difcoveries, and the Arts with new inventions and improvements.

SECTION

# SECTION II.

OF

## ORIGINAL PHILOSOPHIC

# GENIUS.

THE empire of Genius is unbounded. All the Sciences and Arts prefent a fphere for its exercife, and afford fcope for its exertion. But though it may be exerted indifcriminately in all, it will not be exerted equally in each. It will fometimes appear more, fometimes lefs remarkably. Our prefent inquiry leads us to confider how and in what degree original Genius will difplay itfelf in philofophical Science. In order to perceive this, it may not be improper to confider the peculiar province of the Philofopher, and the objects he has in view. His province is to furvey with attention

tention the various phenomena of the natural and moral world, and, with perfpicacity of difcernment, to explore their caufes;
proceeding in his inquiry from the knowledge of effects to the inveftigation of the
caufes by which they were produced. The
objects he has, or ought to have in view,
are, to bring into open light thofe truths
that are wrapped in the fhades of obfcurity,
or involved in the mazes of error, and to apply them to the purpofe of promoting the
happinefs of mankind *.

From

---

* CICERO reprefents it as the peculiar excellence of
the *Socratic* Philofophy, that it had a ftrict connection
with life and manners; and that it was employed on
objects of the utmoft importance to human felicity, on
good and evil, on virtue and vice:

Socrates primus Philofophiam devocavit e cœlo, & in
urbibus collocavit, & in domos etiam introduxit, &
coegit de vita & moribus, rebusque bonis & malis quæ-
rere. *Tufc. Quæft.* lib. v. n. 10.

He obferves, in another part of his Works, that
SOCRATES had difintangled Philofophy from abftrufe
fpe-

From this idea of the objects and province of the Philofopher, the intelligent Reader will, upon a little reflection, clearly perceive that vigorous and extenfive powers of Imagination are indifpenfibly neceffary to enable him to proceed fuccefsfully in the refearches of Science. In order however to make this ftill more evident, let it be obferved, that as it is the proper office of this faculty to affemble thofe ideas, whofe relations to the fubject it contemplates, and to each other, can alone be determined by the faculty of Judgment; fo there are fome of thefe fo obvious, that they occur to common

---

fpeculations, and applied it to the purpofes of common life.

Socrates mihi videtur, id quod conftat inter omnes, primus a rebus occultis, & ab ipfa natura involutis, in quibus omnes ante eum philofophi occupati fuerunt, avocaviffe philofophiam, & ad vitam communem adduxiffe; ut de virtutibus & vitiis omninoque de bonis rebus & malis quæreret; cœleftia autem, vel procul effe a noftra cognitione cenferet, vel fi maxime cognita effent, nihil tamen ad bene vivendum conferre. *Acad.* *Quæft.* lib. i. n. 15.

reflec-

reflection, and arife from the general laws
of affociation, while others are fo far removed beyond the fphere of the common talents allotted to mankind, that they can neither be affembled nor compared, without
fuch an extraordinary proportion of the
powers of Imagination and Reafon, as is
rarely united in one perfon. The power
of affembling and comparing fuch ideas,
in order to determine their relations and
refemblances, is the diftinguifhing characteriftic of an Original Philofophic Genius.

We have formerly obferved, that the faculty of the mind, which we diftinguifh by
the name of Imagination, difcovers itfelf in
a furprifing variety of forms.  To create
uncommon fcenery, to invent new incidents and characters in Poetry, and new
theories in Philofophy; to affociate and
compound, to divide and transform the ideas
of the mind, is the work of one and the
fame power; but is not in all thefe cafes
executed with equal eafe, or with equal
                                    fuccefs.

fuccefs. To invent and create, muft undoubtedly require the higheft exertion of the
faculty we are fpeaking of; becaufe the objects on which the mind employs itfelf in
this exercife, are very remote from common
obfervation, and cannot be brought into
view without a ftrenuous effort of imagination. Hence it happens, that as invention
is the province of original Genius, both in
Philofophy and in Poetry, a very great,
though not a precifely equal or fimilar fhare
of Imagination, is neceffary in each of them.
It will be no incurious employment to obferve the various exertions of the fame faculty in thefe different departments, as it
will open to us an agreeable profpect of the
furprifing verfatility, extent, and vigour of
the human mind; and will alfo enable us
to form a comparative idea of the degree of
Imagination neceffary to confummate original Philofophic Genius.

The inventive faculty difplays itfelf in
Philofophy with great force and extent. It
enables

enables the Philosopher, by its active, vigorous, and exploring power, to conjecture
shrewdly, if not to comprehend fully, the
various springs which actuate the visible
system of Nature and Providence; to frame
the most ingenious theories for the solution
of natural Phenomena; to invent Systems,
and to new-model the natural and moral
World to his own mind. It is intensely ex-
ercised in all this process, as it exerts both a
creative and combining power; which, by
inventing new hypotheses, by connecting
every intermediate and corresponding idea,
and by uniting the several detached parts
of one theorem, rears a fabric of its own,
whose symmetry, justness and solidity, it is
the business of the reasoning faculty to determine.

The kind of Imagination most properly
adapted to Original Philosophic Genius, is
that which is distinguished by REGULARITY,
CLEARNESS, and ACCURACY. The kind peculiar to Original Genius in Poetry, is that
whose

whofe effential properties are a noble IRRE-
GULARITY, VEHEMENCE, and ENTHUSIASM.
Or, to fet the difference betwixt philofophic
and poetic Imagination in another light by
the ufe of an image, we may obferve, that
in the mind of the Philofopher the RAYS of
fancy are more COLLECTED, and more CON-
CENTRATED in one point; and confequently
are more favourable to ACCURATE and DIS-
TINCT VISION: that in the mind of the
Poet they are more DIFFUSED; and therefore their luftre is lefs PIERCING, though
more UNIVERSAL. The former perceives
the objects he contemplates more CLEARLY;
the latter comprehends a greater number of
them at ONE GLANCE. Such are the refpective characters of Imagination in Philofophy and in Poetry, as diftinguifhed from
each other.

As we have already obferved, that an
exact equilibrium of the reafoning and inventive powers of the mind feems to be, in
a great meafure, incompatible with their

H                              very

very oppofite natures, and perhaps was never beftowed on any individual ; the only queftion is, in what proportion thofe powers fhould be diftributed, in order to the intire confummation of original philofophic Genius.

If the pofition we have laid down, and endeavoured to fupport in a preceding fection, fhall be found to be juft, That Imagination is the diftinguifhing ingredient in every kind and degree of Genius, it will obvioufly follow, that this quality muft predominate in the accomplifhment of original Philofophic, as well as Poetic Genius. Indeed, with regard to its predominance in the latter, there will be no difpute. Imagination has by far the greateft fhare of merit in poetical productions. It at once defigns and executes them, calling in only the affiftance of Judgment and Tafte, in order to determine whether it has beftowed on the feveral figures their true proportions, and juft degrees of light and fhade. Were we to invert

vert the cafe, and to fuppofe Judgment the diftinguifhing faculty of the Poet, his productions, it is true, might be more regular and correct; but it is evident, they would be defective in their moft effential excellencies in FICTION and in FIRE.

With regard to ORIGINAL PHILOSOPHIC GENIUS, it feems to be generally imagined, that Judgment is its principal ingredient. As this opinion ftrikes at the foundation of our theory, it will be neceffary to examine it with fome attention.

Let it be obferved therefore, that as Invention is the peculiar and diftinguifhing province of every fpecies of Genius, Imagination claims an undivided empire over this province. It is this faculty alone, which, without the aid or participation of Judgment, fupplies all the incidents, characters, imagery, fentiments, and defcriptions of Poetry, and moft of the theories, at leaft, in Philofophy, as well as the arguments (a

cir-

circumftance not commonly attended to) for fupporting thofe theories. Judgment only claims the right of determining their propriety and truth. Since therefore, to fupply thefe, conftitutes the higheft effort of Genius; that faculty which fupplies them; muft certainly predominate in its full accomplifhment; and this, we have feen, is Imagination. There are at the fame time inferior degrees of Philofophic Genius, in which Judgment has the principal afcendant. Thofe perfons in whom this diftribution takes place, are in general qualified for making improvements in Philofophy, in exact proportion to the degree in which they poffefs the talent of Imagination; and will, upon account of the fuperior ftrength of their reafoning talents, be found better qualified for canvaffing the difcoveries of others, poffeffed of more extenfive powers of Imagination, though perhaps of a lefs penetrating Judgment, than for making thofe difcoveries themfelves. It is true indeed, that befides thofe philofophical truths, which, to the

mor-

mortification of the pride of human underftanding, accident hath brought to light,
and thofe others which have been hit upon
by certain happy random thoughts of perfons of very moderate abilities, difcoveries in
Science have fometimes been made by thofe,
who, enjoying a very fmall fhare of imagination, were however endued with a clear
apprehenfion, united with a patient and
careful obfervation of the various objects
they contemplated. It muft likewife be confeffed, that this method, accompanied with
proper experiments, and juft reafoning founded on thofe experiments, though not the moft
expeditious, is however the only certain one
of attaining the knowledge of the truths of
natural Philofophy in particular. But then,
on the other hand, it muft be acknowledged,
that where an extenfive Imagination is fu-
peradded to the qualifications above-mentioned, the mind, being thereby enabled to
comprehend a greater variety of objects, and
to combine its ideas in a greater variety of
forms, becomes qualified to pufh its inqui-

H 3                                              ries

ries much farther, as well as with more advantage.

After all, though Imagination muſt ever be the predominating ingredient in the INTIRE accompliſhment of ORIGINAL PHILOSOPHIC GENIUS, yet the powers of REASON muſt likewiſe exiſt very NEARLY in an equal degree, in order to its COMPLETE conſummation, and the attainment of the objects it has in view; for if we ſhould ſuppoſe Imagination to predominate in a HIGH degree over the other mental faculties, the conſequence would be, that the Philoſopher in whom it thus predominated, would be perpetually employed in forming ingenious indeed, but extravagant theories, of which his compoſitions would take a deep tincture; and we ſhould be amuſed with the DREAMS of a ROMANTIC viſionary, inſtead of being inſtructed in the TRUTHS of SOUND Philoſophy.

Upon

Upon the whole: as both thefe faculties, united in a high degree, muft concur in forming the truly ORIGINAL PHILOSOPHIC GENIUS, they muft always go hand in hand together in philofophical inquiries, as well as exift almoft, though not altogether, in an equal proportion.

Thus we have fhewn how and by what particular exertions original Genius difcovers itfelf in Philofophy; and have pointed out its fingular efficacy in extending the empire of Science, We have alfo confidered the kind and degree of Imagination peculiarly adapted to ORIGINAL PHILOSOPHIC GENIUS, compared with the kind and degree of the fame quality requifite to ORIGINAL GENIUS in Poetry; at the fame time that we have fhewn, that Imagination ought to predominate in the former as well as the latter. We fhall now conclude this fection with a few flight ftrictures on the characters of fome of the moft diftinguifhed original Authors in phi-

H 4                lofophical

losophical Science, by way of illustrating
the above remarks.

Of all the Philosophers of antiquity,
PLATO possessed the most copious and exuberant imagination, which, joined to a certain contemplative turn of mind, qualified
him for the successful pursuit of philosophi-
cal studies, and enabled him to acquire an
extraordinary eminence in those various
branches of Science, to which he applied
his divine Genius.   He is the only prose
writer, who in Philosophy has dared to
emulate the sublime majesty of the *Mæonian*
Bard †.   He was indeed animated with all
that ardor and enthusiasm of Imagination
which distinguishes the Poet ; and it is impossible for a person, possessed of any degree
of sensibility, to read his Writings without
catching somewhat of the enthusiasm.   The

† Παντων δε τυτων μαλιϛα ὁ Πλατων, απο τυ Ομηρικυ
εκεινυ ϝαματος εις αὑτον μυριας οϛας παρατροπας αποχιτευϛα-
μενος.  LONG. *de Sub.* cap. 13.

Philosophy

Philofophy of PLATO, more than that of
any other, is calculated to elevate and to expand the foul; to fettle, to footh, to refine
the paffions; and to warm the heart with
the love of virtue. Such were the objects of
this amiable Philofopher; and fuch is the
tendency of his doctrine. At prefent we
confider his doctrine merely as a proof of
his Genius. With this view we may obferve, that his fublime contemplations concerning the το ον and the το ἕν *, the exiftence

---

* Thofe who are defirous to know PLATO's fentiments on the exiftence and unity of the Divine Nature,
may confult his *Philebus*, the fifth and fixth books of
his *Republic*, and his *Parmenides*; in all which they
will find the reafoning very fubtile; and in fome places,
particularly through moft of the laft mentioned dialogue, it muft be confeffed, very intricate. For this
reafon, we choofe rather to refer the Reader to thofe
parts of PLATO's Works, where his fentiments on the
above-mentioned fubjects are contained, than to prefent him with a few detached paffages, which could
convey no diftinct idea of his meaning, where the
chain of argumentation is fo ftrictly connected. We
fhall only obferve, that though PLATO fometimes
speaks

ence and unity of the fupreme Being, as
well as the † perfections and providence
of

---

fpeaks agreeably to the eftablifhed mythology of his
country, yet when he intends to deliver his genuine
fentiments, he maintains the abfolute Sovereignty and
Unity of the Deity.

† PLATO, in his *Politicus*, after delivering an ingenious, however unphilofophical a theory, concerning
the various transformations and revolutions the world
had undergone; and after having reprefented it as de-
cayed and worn out in the courfe of fo many tranfmu-
tations, as well as in danger of immediate diffolution,
upon account of the diforder into which its different
parts had been thrown, defcribes the Deity, with great
fublimity, as rifing from his feat of contemplation, re-
fuming the reins of government, prefiding at the helm,
arranging the disjointed parts of the vaft machine of
the world, reftoring them to their primitive order and
beauty, and beftowing upon the whole renewed vigour
and immortality. As this paffage gives a noble idea of
the omnipotence of the Deity, we fhall prefent the
Reader with it.

Διο δη και τοτ' ηδη θιος ὁ κοσμησας αυτον, καθορων εν απορiαις
οντα, κηδομενος ἱνα μη χειμασθις, ὑπο ταραχης διαλυθεις, εις
τον της ανομοιοτητος απειρον οντα τοπον δυη παλιν εφεδρος αυτα
των πηδαλιων γιγνομενος, τα νοσαντα και λυθιντα εν τη καθ'
αυτον

of the Deity; that his theory concerning the caufes, firft principles, and generation of

---

αυτον προτερα περιοδω τριψας, κοσμει τι και επανορθων, αθα-
νοτον αυτον και αγηρω απεργαζεται. Edit. Mars. Ficin.
p. 538.

Our Philofopher, expreffing his own opinion, by the mouth of the *Ælian* Gueft, attributes the creation of all things, even of the materials of which he fuppofes the animal world to be framed, to one fupreme Being:

Ημεις μεν που και τ' αλλα ζωα, και εξ ων τα πεφυκοτ' ιςι, πυρ
και υδωρ και τα τουτων αδελφα, θευ γεννημα τα παντα, ισμεν
αυτα απειργασμενα εκαςα? *Soph.* p. 185.

At the end of his *Timæus*, he reprefents the world as the intelligent, moft perfect image of the Deity:

Θνητα γαρ και α θανατα ζωα λαβων, και ξυμπληρωθεις οδε ο
κοσμος, ουτω ζωον ορατον, τα ορατα περιεχον, εικων τε νοητε
θεε, αισθητος, μεγιςος και αριςος καλλιςος τε και τελεωτατος
γεγονεν, εις ουρανος οδε, μονογενης ων. *Tim.* p. 1089.

And in the fame dialogue he lays it down as an indifputable maxim, that God made all things perfect in their kind:

Το δε η δυνατον ως καλλιςα τε και αριςα εξ ουχ ουτως εχοντων,
τον θεον αυτα ξυνιςαναι περι παντα ημιν ως αει τετο λεγομενον
υπαρχιτω. p. 1062.

In

of things, and the foul which animates and actuates the whole frame of Nature \*; his fentiments concerning virtue,

In other paffages, PLATO celebrates the moral as well as natural perfections of the Deity. Thus he reprefents him as the complete model of juftice.

ΘιΘ· ουδαμη ουδαμως αδικΘ·, αλλ ὡς οιον τι δικαιοταῖΘ·. και ὰκ ιςιν αυτω ὁμοιοτιρον ὰδιν η ὁς αν ημων αυ γιινηται ὁ τι δικαιοταῖΘ·. Theæt. p. 129.

He makes SOCRATES likewife ftrongly affert the doctrine of a particular Providence, exercifed in favour of good men. This laft, addreffing himfelf to fuch of his judges as had vindicated his innocence, makes the following declaration :

Αλλα και υμιις χρη ω ανδις δικαςαι, ιυιλπιδας ιιναι πρΘ· τον θανατον. και ιν τι τὰτο διανοιιδαι, αληθις ὁτι ὰκ ιςι ανδρι αγαθω κακον ὰδιν ουτι ζων τι, ουτι τιλιυτησαντι. Apoll. Socrat. p. 31.

\* PLATO's doctrines concerning the *Anima Mundi*, the Soul of the World, the caufes, original principles, and formation of things, the revolutions of matter, and tranfmigration of fouls, are among the profound myfteries of his Philofophy. Speaking of the *Anima Mundi*, as infufed by the Deity, he tells us ;

Ψυχ̀ν

ture * ; and the happinefs of thofe fouls
who are gradually appropriated to the fo-

---

Ψυχην δε ιις το μισον αυτε Θεις, δια παν]Θ- τι ετεινε, και ετι εξω
το σωμα αυτη περιεκαλυψε, και κυκλω δη κυκλον ςριφομενον,
ουρανον ινα μονον ερημον κατιςησι. *Tim.* p. 1049.

Thofe who are defirous of obtaining full fatisfaction
on this and the above-mentioned fubjects, may confult
the *Timæus,* where they will find them particularly
treated ; and where they will be entertained with a variety of notions ftrangely fanciful, indicating the inexhauftible fecundity of Imagination peculiar to this
great Philofopher.


\* PLATO confiders virtue in feveral different lights ;
fubftituting fome of its particular and effential ingredients in place of the general quality which they conftitute. Thus he fubftitutes juftice at one time for
this quality, at another, temperance, at another, forti-
tude ; but pofitively maintains that it cannot be taught,
but muft be implanted in the mind by divine fate ; an
opinion which gives us a very fublime idea of the nature of virtue :

Ει δε νυν ημεις εν παντι τω λογω τουτω καλως εζητησαμεν τε
και ελεγομεν, αριτη αν ειη ουτε φυσιι, ουτε διδακτον· αλλα θεια
μοιρα παραγιγνομενη ανευ νου, οις αν παρα γιγηηται. *Meno*,
p. 427.

vereign

vereign good and the supreme beauty †
that his reflections on prayer *, and on divine

---

† In speaking of the sovereign good and supreme
beauty, he breaks out into a kind of divine enthusiasm, which absorbs his mental faculties in rapturous
admiration and love of that glorious Object, which
his ardent Imagination had represented as inexpressi-
bly amiable:

Τι δητα (ιφη) οιομιθα, ειτω γινοιτο αυτο το καλον ιδειν ειλικρι-
νες, καθαρον, αμικτον, αλλ᾽ α μη αναπλιων σαρκων τι ανθρωπι-
νων και χρωματων, και αλλης πολλης φλυαριας θνητης, αλλ᾽
αυτο το θιιον, καλον δυναιτο μονοιιδες κατιδειν; αρ᾽ οιι (ιφη)
φαυλον βιον γιγνεσθαι ικιισι βλιπον]Ͼ ανθρωπυ, και ικιινο ὁ διι
θιωμινου και ξυνον]Ͼ αυτω; η υκ ινθυμη (ιφη) ὁτι ινταυθα
αυτω μοναχη γινηςιται, ορωντι ὡ ορατον το καλον, τικτιιν υκ
ειδωλα αριτης ατι υκ ειδωλα ιφαπτομινω; αλλ᾽ αληθη, ατι τυ
αληθυς ιφαπτομινω; τικοντι δε αριτην αληθη, και θριψαμινω,
ψπαρχιι θιοφιλιι γινεσθαι, και ειπιρ τω αλλω ανθρωπω, αθανατω
και ικιινω. Sympos. p. 1199.

---

* It is pretty generally known, that the nature and
qualifications of the duty of prayer, compose the subject of the second ALCIBIADES. SOCRATES, having
convinced this young hero of the absurdity, as well as
impiety of addressing the Gods rashly, recommends
that form of prayer used by a certain Poet:

vine love and friendſhip †, are ſtriking in-
ſtances of the fertility of our Philoſopher's
imagination,

---

Ζευ βασιλευ, τα μεν εϑλα και ευχομενοις και ανευκτοις
Αμμι διδϑ, τα δε δεινα και ευχομενοις απαλιξιιν κελευιι.

P. 454.

Having impreſſed upon the mind of ALCIBIADES a
deep ſenſe of the importance of the duty of prayer, in
which he was going to engage, and at the ſame time
ſhewn him how apt moſt men were, from their ignorance of what was really good for them, to aſk from
the Gods, what, if granted, might prove highly de-
ſtructive to themſelves; he obſerves, that it becomes
us to conſider well, before we addreſs thoſe ſuperior
Beings, what we ought, and what we ought not to
ſay:

Αλλα δοκει μοι πολλης φυλακης δειϑαι και σκεψεως, ο, τι ποτε
ρητεον εςι και μη. P. 458.

And a little after, from the conſideration of our own
ignorance, he infers the neceſſity of waiting for divine
Illumination, in order to enable us to perform the duty
of prayer properly:

Αναγκαιον ϑν ιςι περιμενειν εως αν τις μαθη ως δει προς ϑεους και
προς ανθρωπους διακειϑαι.

† In the dialogue, intitled *Lyſis*, PLATO gives us the
opinion of his Maſter concerning the nature of friendſhip.

imagination, as well as of that moral and speculative difpofition, which we have elfe-where obferved to diftinguifh Philofophic Genius *.

It will perhaps be alledged, that the moft fublime notions in PLATO's Philofophy were originally derived from divine revelation, and that he had little elfe than the merit of collecting and forming them into a fyftem. This point GALE, in his *Court of the Gentiles*,

---

fhip. SOCRATES, intending to reclaim the unhappy youth from whom the dialogue takes its name, from thofe criminal indulgences into which he was in hazard of being betrayed, leads him, ftep by ftep, from the means to the end, from the confideration of inferior enjoyments to the contemplation of the SOVEREIGN, ULTIMATE, and UNCREATED GOOD, in which all fubordinate gratifications ought to center, and on which our moft ardent affections ought to be fixed:

Αρ ϑι ϰ αναγκη απιπιιν ημας ϑυτως ιοιτας, και αϕιϰιϑαι επι τιια ϑρχην, η ϰ επαιοισει επ' αλλο Φιλον, αλλ' ηξιι ιπ' εϰειιο ὸ ιϛι πρωτον Φιλον. ὁυ ειεϰα και τα αλλα Φαμιν παιτα Φιλα ιιιαι. *Lyfis*, p. 507.

* Book I. Sect. 2.

hath

hath laboured to prove. It muft indeed be confeffed, that PLATO enjoyed great advantages, and was favoured with peculiar means and opportunities of acquiring knowledge, which he did not fail to improve. Having travelled into *Egypt* and *Italy*, he made himfelf acquainted with the myfteries of the *Egyptian* Priefts, as well as with the more fecret and profound doctrines of the *Pythagorean* School; and no doubt by tradition, however corrupted and interpolated, he might obtain fome very imperfect knowledge of the fundamental principles of the Jewifh religion. Indeed the ftrong refemblance betwixt the doctrines of PLATO, and thofe contained in the Old Teftament, renders this conjecture highly probable. At the fame time it appears equally probable, that as others are very different both from the Sacred and *Pythagorean* doctrines, they are properly derived from neither, but are the production of his own inventive Genius.

DES CARTES, the *French* Philofopher, had
the honour of firft reforming the Philofophy
of his country. He ftruck out a path for
himfelf, through the gloom which the obfcure and unintelligible jargon of the Schools
had thrown on Science; and though he
could not purfue it through its feveral wind-
ings, he pointed out the track which has
been followed by others, and has led to the
moft important difcoveries. He inherited
from nature a ftrong and vivid Imagination; but the too great predominance and
indulgence of this very faculty, was the caufe
of all thofe errors in Philofophy into which
he was betrayed. His theories of the different vortices of the heavenly bodies, and
of that immenfe whirlpool of fluid matter,
through which, in confequence of an original impulfe, they are fuppofed to revolve, have, by our celebrated NEWTON,
been fhewn to be falfe; though thofe
theories are a proof of the creative Imagination of their Author; but of an imagination too freely indulged, and too little
fub-

subjected to the prudent reftraints of Judgment.

What Des Cartes was to the *French*,
Lord Bacon was to the *English* nation.
He was indeed not only the reformer, but
the reviver and reftorer of Learning.   As
his penetrating and comprehenfive Genius *
enabled

---

* Perhaps no age or nation can boaft of having produced a more comprehenfive and univerfal Genius,
than that which Lord Bacon feems to have poffeffed.
He applied his Genius to almoft every department of
Literature and Science, and fucceeded in every fphere
which he attempted.   Human knowledge was divided
by him into three diftinct branches, Hiftory, Poetry,
and Philofophy (vid. *de Aug. Scient.* fect. 1.) the firft relating to the Memory, the fecond to the Imagination,
and the laft to Reafon or the Judgment.   With refpect
to Philofophy, inftead of employing his imagination in
framing air-built theories, he began his inquiries into
the works of nature, with laying it down as a fundamental maxim, that man knows juft as much only of
the courfe of nature, as he has learned from obfervation
and experience : " Homo naturæ minifter & interpres,
" tantum facit & intelligit, quantum de naturæ ordine,
" re vel mente obfervaverit, nec amplius fcit aut poteft,"

enabled him to difcern and expofe the errors
of the Scholaftic Philofophy; fo it qualified
him not only for extending the empire of
Science far beyond the limits within which
it had been formerly confined, but alfo for
difcovering thofe immenfe tracts of uncultivated ground, which fince his time, by
tracing his footfteps, have been occupied and
improved. He had the honour of introducing experimental Philofophy *, and fucceeded

---

(*Nov. Org.* lib. i. aph. 1.) and upon this juft axiom, the
refult of mature reflection and good fenfe, he founded
all his philofophical difcoveries.

* When we affirm that Lord BACON introduced
experimental Philofophy into his country, we do not
mean to affert, that its ufe was wholly unknown before
his time; but that he was the firft who taught and re-
gularly practifed the method of inveftigating the caufes
of the phenomena of nature by certain experiments.
The excellence and advantage of this method of inveftigation he celebrates very juftly : " Sed demonftratio
" longe optima eft *experientia*; modo hæreat in ipfo
" *experimento.* Nam fi traducatur ad alia quæ *fimilia*
" exiftimantur, nifi *rite & ordine* fiat illa traductio res
" *fallax* eft." (*Ibid.* fect. 70.) After which he cen-
fures

ceeded in many of the experiments which he made. Thofe particularly, in which, by the help of a pneumatic engine he had himfelf contrived, he endeavoured to difcover the weight and elafticity of the air, in which he was to a great degree fuccefsful, though the above-mentioned properties were more minutely calculated afterwards, do abundance of credit to his philofophical fagacity. His moral Effays, his book *de Augmentis Scientiarum* *,

his

---

fures the *partial*, *inaccurate*, and *cafual* method of making experiments in his own time ; in oppofition to which he points out the true procefs to be obferved by the Philofopher, who afpires to the honour of extending the limits of human knowledge : " At contra verus " experientiæ ordo primum lumen accendit, deinde " per lumen iter demonftrat, incipiendo ab experien- " tia ordinata & digefta, & minime præpoftera aut er- " ratica, atque ex ea educendo axiomata, atque ex " axiomatibus conftitutis rurfus experimenta nova." *(Ibid.)*

* The defign of the book *de Augmentis Scientiarum,* is to take a general furvey of human knowledge, divide it into its feveral branches, obferve the deficiencies in thofe branches, and fuggeft the methods by

which

his *Novum Organum* †, and his treatifes of Phyfics and Natural Hiftory ‡, have gained him great reputation ; as indeed all his works are a proof of his having poffeffed that nice

---

which they may be fupplied ; an undertaking executed in a great meafure by the Author himfelf in fome following tracts.

† In the *Novum Organum Scientiarum*, the Author points out the caufes of ignorance and error in the Sciences, at the fame time that he lays down certain aphorifms, founded on perception and confcioufnefs, or deduced from obfervation and experience, as fo many fteps in the intellectual fcale, by which we may rife to the knowledge of univerfal truths. Thofe leading difquifitions and experiments are likewife pointed out, which open to us the moft comprehenfive views of the works of nature, as well as facilitate the inventions and improvements of the arts.

‡ The Author, in his *Sylva Sylvarum*, attempts a kind of hiftory of nature and art ; enumerates many of the phenomena of the univerfe for this purpofe, which he calls the third part of his Inftauration ; and in the fourth part of this Work, denominated *Scala Intellectus*, he fhews the method of employing the materials of the *Sylva Sylvarum*, by a variety of examples, fuch as his Hiftory of Life and Death, his Hiftory of the Winds, and his Condenfation and Rarefaction of natural Bodies.

tem-

temperature of Imagination and Judgment, which conftitute truly original Philofophic Genius.

In adducing examples of this quality, it would be inexcufable to omit mentioning Sir ISAAC NEWTON, a name fo revered by Mathematicians and Philofophers of every degree. This great man was doubtlefs in Philofophy an original Genius of the firft rank. His various and ftupendous difcoveries of the revolutions of the heavenly bodies, as well as of the laws by which thofe revolutions are regulated; of their feveral magnitudes, orbits, and diftances; and of that great and fundamental law of attraction, by which all nature is fupported and actuated; his theory of light, as an emanation from the fun; his calculation of its rapidity, and of the reflection and refrangibility of its rays; his fubtil and curious anatomy of thofe rays, and the divifion and arrangement of the elementary ones which compofe them, together with their union

I 4

in

in the formation of colours, are the moſt
aſtoniſhing efforts of the human mind; and
while they ſhew the prodigious compaſs of
that imagination, which could frame and
comprehend ſuch ſublime conceptions, they
at the ſame time clearly evince the profound
depth of penetration and ſtrength of reaſon, which, by a kind of divine intuition,
could diſcern and demonſtrate their truth.

Doctor BERKELEY, Biſhop of *Cloyne*, was
another original philoſophic Genius of dis-
tinguiſhed eminence.  While HOBBES and
SPINOZA maintained the doctrine of abſolute materialiſm, admitting nothing but
matter, in one form or another, in the uni-
verſe, BERKELEY excluded it altogether from
his ſyſtem, and denied its exiſtence out of a
mind perceiving it.   A doctrine ſo new and
uncommon, and ſeemingly ſo contrary to
the evidence of our ſenſes, could not fail at
firſt to raiſe aſtoniſhment, and to meet with
oppoſition : yet this ingenious Author has
ſupported his theory by ſuch plauſible arguments,

ments, that many perfons appear to be convinced by them, and to have adopted his
fentiments. The truth is, though, relying
on the teftimony of our fenfes, we allow
the real exiftence of matter, and are fufficiently acquainted with its effential properties, folidity, extenfion, and divifibility; yet
its genuine effence, or the fubftratum in
which thofe properties exift, is ftill a myftery
to Philofophers, and will probably continue
to be fo. Whether the above-mentioned
tenet of this Author fhould be generally received as an eftablifhed article in the Philofopher's Creed, or not, it muft, fupported
as it is with fuch ftrength of reafon and invention, undoubtedly be confidered as a fignal proof of his having poffeffed a very high
degree of original Philofophic Genius.

The laft original Genius in Philofophy,
we fhall take notice of, is BURNET, the Author of *the Theory of the Earth*; a fyftem fo
new, fo confiftent, and conceived with fuch
ftrength of fancy, that one is almoft tempted

**to**

to be of the same opinion with the Author
of *the Essay on the Writings and Genius of*
Pope, who hath ventured to declare, that in
this admirable performance, there appears a
degree of Imagination little inferior to what
is discovered in *Paradise Lost*. His hypotheses of the position and form of the ante-
diluvian earth, of the causes which produced
the universal deluge, occasioned by the opening of the floodgates of Heaven, aided by the
bursting asunder of the frame of the earth,
and its falling into the great abyss, with
which it was surrounded, and on which it as
it were floated; his opinions of the paradi-
siacal state, of the agreeable temperature of
its seasons, and of the peculiar beauties of
this primeval constitution of nature; his
theory of the general conflagration, its causes
and progress, and of the universal judgment
consequent upon it, together with his idea of
the nature, happiness, and time of the Mil-
lenium, form altogether such a surprising,
ingenious, and at the same time, not improbable system, that we cannot help ad-
miring

miring the whole as the production of an inventive and truly creative Genius.

Thefe examples, we hope, will be fufficient to fhew the importance, the ufe, and the fphere of Imagination in philofophical dis-quifitions; and to point out thofe particular degrees, and that happy temperature of Ima-gination and Judgment, which conftitute and accomplifh original Philofophic Genius. Many other diftinguifhed names in Philofo-phy might have been added to thofe above-mentioned; but as the narrow limits of our plan, on this branch of the fubject, do not allow our running out to greater length in the way of illuftration, fo the adducing more examples, in order to confirm the pre-ceding remarks, will, we imagine, after thofe already adduced, be altogether unneceffary.

SECTION

# SECTION III.

OF

ORIGINAL

GENIUS

IN

# POETRY.

P OETRY *, of all the liberal Arts, affords the moſt extenſive ſcope for the

---

* ARISTOTLE, inquiring into the origin of Poetry, aſſigns two principal cauſes of it, a natural DESIRE of IMITATION, and the pleaſure ariſing from the ſucceſs of that IMITATION:

Εοικασι δε γεννησαι μεν όλως την ποιητικην αιτιαι δυο τινες, και αυται φυσικαι. Το, τι γαρ μιμεισθαι, συμφυτον τοις αν- θρωποις εκ παιδων εστι, και τυτω διαφερυσι των αλλων ζωων, οτι μιμη-

the difplay of a Genius truly Original. In Philofophy, the empire of Imagination, and confequently of Genius, is in fome degree neceffarily reftricted; in Poetry, it is altogether abfolute and unconfined. To accomplifh the Philofopher, who would make new difcoveries in Science, a large proportion of Imagination is (as we have already fhewn) undoubtedly requifite; but to conftitute the true Poet, the higheft degree of this quality is indifpenfibly neceffary. Smooth verfification and harmonious numbers will no more make genuine Poetry, than the atoms of a fkeleton put together can make an animated and living figure. To produce either, a certain vital fpirit muft be infufed; and in Poetry, this vital fpirit is INVENTION †. By this

---

μιμητικωτατον ιςι, και τας μαθησεις ποιιται δια μιμησιως τας ιρωτας, και το χαιριιν τοις μιμημασι παντας. *Arif. Poet.* cap. 4.

† The fame great Critic obferves, that as it is the office of the Hiftorian to relate fuch things as are really done, it is the proper office of the Poet to relate the
kind

this quality it is principally characterifed; which, being the very foul of all poetical compofition, is likewife the fource of that inchanting delight, which the mind receives from its perufal. Invention may be confidered as confifting of INCIDENTS, of CHARACTERS, of IMAGERY, of SENTIMENT; in all which, original poetic Genius will difplay itfelf in an uncommon degree. We fhall confider its efforts in each of thefe feparately.

---

kind of things that fhould be done, according to what is required by neceffity, or the rules of probability:

Φανερὸν δε εκ των ειρημινων, και οτι ε το τα γινομινα λιγιιν, τετο ποιητε εργον εςιν, αλλ οια αν γινοιτο, και τα δυνατα καλα τη εικος, η το αναγκαιον. Ὁ γαρ ἱςορικῷ και ὁ ποιητης, ε τω η εμμιτρα λιγιιν η αμιτρα διαφιρεσιν ειη γαρ αν τα Ἡροδοτε εις μιτρα τιθιναι, και εδιν ητ7ον αν ειη ἱςορια τις μιτα μιτρε η ανυ μιτρων αλλα τετω διαφιρει τω τον μιν τα γινομινα λιγιιν, τον δι οια αν γινοιτο. *Ibid.* cap. 9.

In order however to relate the kind of things that fhould be done, the Poet muft poffefs the power of Invention.

First,

Firſt, in the invention of INCIDENTS. Some incidents are ſo obvious, that by a natural aſſociation of ideas, they inſtantly occur to the mind of every one poſſeſſed of ordinary abilities, and are very eaſily conceived. Others however are more remote, and lie far beyond the reach of ordinary faculties *; coming only within the verge of thoſe

---

* A perſon who is deſtitute of Imagination, muſt neceſſarily regard a ſeries of fictitious incidents, which are at the ſame time ſurpriſing and important, with great aſtoniſhment; and he will feel it extremely difficult to conceive them to have been invented by the mere fertility of the Poet's fancy. The reaſon of both ſeems to be this: Such a perſon, having ſcarce any other ideas than what ariſe from ſenſation, and the moſt common laws of aſſociation, will be apt to ſuppoſe that all mankind receive their ideas by the ſame modes of conveyance; being ignorant of thoſe exquiſitely nice relations of ideas reſulting from certain laws of combination that do not operate upon his own mind, but which, operating upon minds of a finer frame, are the ſource of that rich fund of Invention which he admires, but can ſcarce comprehend. Senſation and reflection are indeed the common fountains of all our ideas and all our knowledge; but when once thoſe ideas are conveyed into the mind by means of the
ſenſes,

thofe few perfons, whofe minds are capacious enough to contain that prodigious croud of ideas, which an extenfive obfervation and experience fupply; whofe underftandings are penetrating enough to difcover the moft diftant connections of thofe ideas, and whofe imaginations are fufficiently quick, in combining them at pleafure. It is this kind of incidents which original Genius delights to invent; incidents which are in themfelves great as well as uncommon. Let it not however be fuppofed, that the invention even of thefe is a laborious employment to a Writer of this ftamp; for it is the prerogative of a great Genius to think and to write with eafe, very rarely, if ever, expe-

---

fenfes, they undergo an infinite variety of modification in the mind of a man of Genius, in comparifon of what they admit of in one who is deftitute of this quality. In the former cafe, Imagination, like a grand alembic, gradually refines, and (if I may ufe the expreffion) fublimates thofe conceptions that heretofore participated of the groffnefs of fenfe, from which they were ultimately derived.

riencing

riencing a barrenneſs of Imagination. He has nothing to do but to give ſcope to the excurſions of this faculty, which, by its active and creative power, exploring every receſs of thought, will ſupply an inexhauſtible variety of ſtriking incidents. A facility, therefore, of inventing and combining ſuch incidents in compoſition, may be regarded as one characteriſtical indication of a Genius truly Original *.

The

---

* It is, we believe, commonly ſuppoſed, at leaſt it ſeems to be the opinion of ſome, that the invention of a variety of new and intereſting incidents, is the moſt ſignal proof and exertion of Genius. This opinion, however, though, upon the firſt reflection it has an air of probability, will appear, upon a ſtricter inquiry, to be without any foundation. The invention of characters, which will be afterwards particularly conſidered, is unqueſtionably the greateſt effort of original Genius. In ſupport of this poſition, let it be obſerved, that in this ſpecies of Invention, the mind has a greater diverſity of objects to employ it; and muſt therefore, in order to comprehend them, exert its faculties with vigour, as well as keep them on the ſtretch. Thus, in the exhibition of an uncommon character, the Imagination muſt invent the SENTIMENTS, LANGUAGE,

K                    MANNERS,

The fecond fpecies of invention we mentioned was that of CHARACTERS.    Ordinary

---

MANNERS, and OFFICES peculiar to it, and Judgment
muft determine concerning the PROPRIETY of each;
in the execution of which it is evident, both thefe faculties muft be very INTENSELY exercifed, particularly
the firft; fince to conceive and reprefent characters
which never exifted, but are the pure CREATION of
the mind (for of fuch only we are fpeaking at prefent)
muft indicate the utmoft FERTILITY and FORCE of
Imagination.    On the other hand, though we readily
allow the invention of various, important, and furprifing events, to be a proof of the exiftence of original Genius in a high degree, yet we cannot regard it
as fo remarkable an exertion of this talent, as the invention of uncommon characters; becaufe the imagination of an original Author in Poetry, feeling a native bent to fiction, will, even in its paftime, naturally
run into the firft, as incidents are lefs COMPLICATED,
and therefore more eafily invented than characters;
but it cannot accomplifh the laft without the moft
ftrenuous efforts.    Were we to admit the invention of
furprifing incidents, as the moft diftinguifhing criterion of ORIGINALITY, we fhould be under a neces-
fity of affigning the fuperiority in this refpect to
ARIOSTO, over HOMER and SHAKESPEAR; fince we
find that a much greater variety of events have been
feigned in the *Orlando Furiofo* of the former, than in
all

nary Writers, and even thofe who are pos-
feffed of no inconfiderable talents, commonly
fatisfy themfelves, in this branch of compofition, with copying the characters which
have been drawn by Authors of fuperior
merit, and think they acquit themfelves
fufficiently, when they produce a juft refemblance of the originals they profefs to
imitate. A moderate degree of praife is no
doubt due to fuccefsful imitators; but an
Author of original Genius will not content
himfelf with a mediocrity of reputation;
confcious of the ftrength of his own talents, he difdains to imitate what perhaps
he is qualified to excel. Imitation indeed,
of every kind, except that of nature, has a
tendency to cramp the inventive powers of
the mind, which, if indulged in their excurfions, might difcover new mines of intellectual

---

all the Works of the two laft mentioned Poets put together; a preference furely, which neither the dictates
of impartial Reafon, nor the laws of found Criticifm,
could ever juftify.

K 2

ore, that lie hid only from thofe who are incapable or unwilling to dive into the receffes
in which it lies buried.   A Writer however,
of the kind laft mentioned, inftead of
tracing the footfteps of his predeceffors, will
allow his imagination to range over the field
of Invention, in queft of its materials; and,
from the group of figures collected by it,
will ftrike out a character like his own Genius, perfectly Original.

It may be obferved, that there are three
different kinds of characters, in the invention and reprefentation of which, originality
of Genius may be difcovered with GREAT,
though not with EQUAL advantage.   The
firft of thefe are real human characters, fuch
as are found in every country and age.   The
fecond are likewife human, but of the moft
dignified kind; raifed far above the level of
common life, and peculiar to the pureft and
moft heroic times.   The laft fort of characters is that of beings wholly different in their
natures from mankind; fuch as Ghofts,
Witches,

Witches, Fairies, and the like, which may be termed fupernatural.

Perhaps it may be thought, that in the firft of thefe cafes, Invention has nothing to do, and cannot with any propriety be exercifed; fince to conceive juftly, and to exprefs naturally, are the principal requifites in an Author, who would exhibit a faithful portrait of real charaters. It muft be confeffed, that in this inftance there is not fo much fcope afforded for invention as in the others; nay farther, that it is neceffarily much reftricted. But let it be obferved, that though juft and lively conceptions of the charaters to be reprefented, together with the power of defcribing thofe conceptions, are the qualifications moft effentially requifite to the faithful exhibition of fuch characters, both thefe qualities depend upon the Imagination; for though impartial Judgment muft determine how far the intire refemblance is juft, yet to dictate the fentiments and language, and to furnifh the actions

K 3                          peculiar

peculiar to the different perfons exhibited, is
the work of Invention alone. It will be
readily underftood, that we are at prefent
fpeaking of characters reprefented on the
ftage, and taken from real life, in the defcribing of which we fuppofe an original
Author to employ his Genius †.

The

---

† It cannot be doubted but that Original Genius
may be difcovered in Comedy and works of Humour,
as well as in the higher fpecies of Poetry, thofe of Tragedy and the *Epopœa*; though the originality difcovered
in the firft will be very different, both in kind and degree, from that which is difcovered in the two laft.

Thus the Author of *Hudibras* was in his peculiar
way an Original, as well as the Author of the *Iliad*;
and HOGARTH, in drawing fcenes and characters in
low life, with fuch uncommon propriety, juftnefs and
humour, difcovers a certain ORIGINALITY, though far
inferior IN ITS KIND to what appears in thofe illuftrious
monuments of Genius left us by RAPHAEL URBIN and
MICHAEL ANGELO. There can be no queftion which
of the Poets, or which of the Painters, was the greateft
Genius; for the comparative merit of illuftrious or ingenious Artifts is eftimated, not merely from the EXE-
CUTION. but from the DESIGN, and from the SUBJECT
which employed their pens and pencils. Thus there is

a

The second fort of characters, in the invention and proper reprefentation of which
we

---

a fublimity in the works of the Epic Bard, and in the pieces of the Hiftory Painters above-mentioned, which gives them a vaft fuperiority over thofe of the humorous Poet and ludicrous Artift already named.

We obferved likewife, that the DEGREE of ORIGINALITY which may be difcovered in the higher fpecies of Poetry, is different from that which Comedy admits of. The DEGREE of ORIGINALITY in any performance whatever, depends upon the degree of INVENTION appearing in it; and as there is in general at leaft occafion for a greater proportion of this quality in Tragedy and the *Epopœa*, than in Comedy, we may infer, that a greater degree of ORIGINAL GENIUS is requifite to an excellence in the two firft, than is neceffary to an excellence in the laft. In the former, both the characters and incidents are in a great meafure FICTITIOUS; in the latter, they are for the moft part taken from REAL life; the one fetting before our eyes an illuftrious model of virtue, teaches us what we SHOULD BE; the other prefenting to our view a faithful portrait of our vices and follies, drawn from obfervation, teaches us what WE ARE. Hence it fhould feem, that a SUBLIME and CREATIVE Imagination is neceffary to conftitute a TALENT for Epic Poetry, or for Tragedy; and that a QUICK and LIVELY one, ac-

K 4                     companied

we obferved an original Genius would excel, is that of the moft elevated kind, fuch as is raifed far above the ordinary ftandard of human excellence, yet not altogether above the fphere of humanity; fuch as is not abfolutely unattainable by man, but is rarely found in common life, and is peculiar to the moft heroic ages of the world. It is this kind of characters which is moft fuitable to the dignity of the epic and the tragic Mufe: the latter indeed hath greatly extended her prerogative, by affuming the privilege of reprefenting every kind of diftrefs, and making vicious characters frequently the principal perfonages of the drama. We fhall only by the way obferve on this fubject, that though one end of Tragedy, the exciting of terror, may be anfwered moft effectually by this method, the other ends, namely, the raifing of our admiration and pity, can by no means

---

companied with an extenfive KNOWLEDGE of mankind, is the principal requifite to a MASTERY in Comedy.

be

be accomplifhed by it ; fince to effectuate thefe, virtue muft appear great and venerable in diftrefs. Though virtuous characters labouring under calamities, do at leaft in general afford the moft proper fubjects for Tragedy, as appears from the reafon already given, yet we are far from laying it down as an effential rule, that fuch characters muft always be exhibited in this branch of Poetry; for we are fenfible, that as Tragedy admits of great latitude with regard to the choice of its fubjects, it is a rule which may fometimes with propriety be tranfgreffed ; yet we will lay it down as an inviolable law in the conduct of an Epic Poem, that the characters of the principal perfons muft be virtuous and illuftrious. In reprefenting characters of this kind, whether in Tragedy or the *Epopœa*, an original Genius will difcover the fertility and richnefs of his invention. Finding no characters in real life every way fuited to his purpofe, his Imagination amply fupplies the defect, and enables him to form thofe complete models of excellence, which

neither

neither obfervation nor experience could furnifh. By the creative and combining power of this faculty, he affembles thofe fhining qualities which conftitute the Hero, and exhibits them, united together with per-feft fymmetry, in one ftriking and graceful figure. Inftead of copying the Heroes of HOMER, or of any other Author ancient or modern, he will prefent us with Heroes which are properly his own; being the tranfcripts of thofe models of genuine ex-cellence, which he has formed in his own mind. We do not affirm that fuch charac-ters will be altogether imaginary. The groundwork may be taken from hiftory or tradition, though it is the province of the Poet to finifh the piece; and the Poet that is truly original, will do this with admirable art and invention.

The third and laft fort of charaćters, in which, above all others, an original Genius will moft remarkably difplay his invention, is of that kind which we called PRETERNA-
TURAL,

TURAL, and is altogether different from mere HUMAN characters. Witches, Ghosts, Fairies, and such other unknown visionary beings, are included in the species of which we are speaking. Of the manner of existence, nature and employment of these wonderful beings, we have no certain or determinate ideas. It should seem that our notions of them, vague and indistinct as they are, are derived from tradition and popular opinion; or are the children of Fancy, Superstition, and Fear. These causes concuring with, as well as operating upon, the natural credulity of mankind, have given birth to prodigies and fables concerning " Gorgons, and Hydras, and chimeras dire;" which have been always eagerly swallowed by the vulgar, though they may have been justly rejected by the wise. However averse the latter may be to think with the former on subjects of this kind, it is certain, that their ideas of Ghosts, Witches, Dæmons, and such like apparitions, must be very much the same with theirs,

theirs, fince they draw them from the fame fource, that of traditionary relation; and, how reluctant foever the Judgment may be to yield its affent, the Imagination catches and retains the impreffion, whether we will or not. It is true, the ideas of thofe beings, which are common to all, are very general and obfcure; there is therefore great fcope afforded for the flights of Fancy in this boundlefs region. Much may be invented, and many new ideas of their nature and offices may be acquired. The wildeft and moft exuberant imagination will fucceed beft in excurfions of this kind, " beyond the vifible diurnal fphere," and will make the moft ftupendous difcoveries in its aerial tour. In this region of fiction and fable, original Genius will indulge its adventurous flight without reftraint : it will dart a beam upon the dark fcenes of futurity, draw the veil from the invifible world, and expofe to our aftonifhed view " that undifcovered country, from whofe bourne no traveller returns."

SHAKESPEAR,

SHAKESPEAR, with whofe words we con-
cluded the laft fentence, is the only *Englifh*
writer, who with amazing boldnefs has ventured to burft the barriers of a feparate ftate,
and difclofe the land of Apparitions, Shadows,
and Dreams; and he has nobly fucceeded in
his daring attempt. His very peculiar excellence in this refpect will be more properly
illuftrated in another part of our Effay. In
the mean time we may obferve, that it will
be hazardous for any one to purfue the track
which he has marked out; and that none
but a Genius uncommonly original, can hope
for fuccefs in the purfuit.

Should fuch a Genius arife, he could not
defire a nobler field for the difplay of an exuberant Imagination, than what the fpiritual
world, with its ftrange inhabitants, will
prefent to him. In defcribing the nature
and employment of thofe vifionary beings,
whofe exiftence is fixed in a future ftate, or
of thofe who exift in the prefent, or may
be fuppofed to inhabit the " midway air,"
but

but are poffeffed of certain powers and faculties, very different from what are pos-
feffed by mankind, he is not, as in defcribing human characters, reftricted to exact
probability, much lefs to truth: for we are
in moft inftances utterly ignorant of the
powers of different or fuperior beings; and,
confequently, are very incompetent judges
of the probability or improbability of the
particular influence, or actions attributed to
them.   All that we require of a Poet therefore, who pretends to exhibit characters of
this kind, is, that the incidents, in effectuating which they are fuppofed to be concerned, be poffible, and confonant to the general
analogy of their nature; an analogy, founded
not upon truth or ftrict probability, but
upon common tradition or popular opinion.
It is evident therefore that the Poet, who
would give us a glimpfe of the other world,
and an idea of the nature, employment, and
manner of exiftence of thofe who inhabit it,
or of thofe other imaginary beings, who
are in fome refpects fimilar to, but in others
totally

totally different from mankind, and are fuppofed to dwell on or about this earth, has
abundant fcope for the exercife of the moft
fertile Invention.    This ideal region is indeed the proper fphere of Fancy, in which
fhe may range with a loofe rein, without
fuffering reftraint from the fevere checks of
Judgment ; for Judgment has very little
jurifdiction in this province of Fable.    The
invention of the fupernatural characters
above-mentioned, and the exhibition of
them, with their proper attributes and offices, are the higheft efforts and the moft
pregnant proofs of truly ORIGINAL GENIUS.

The third fpecies of Invention, by which
we obferved original Genius will be diftinguifhed, is that of IMAGERY.    The ftile of
an original Author in Poetry is for the moft
part FIGURATIVE and METAPHORICAL. The
ordinary modes of fpeech being unable to
exprefs the grandeur or the ftrength of his
conceptions, appear FLAT and LANGUID to
his ardent Imagination.    In order therefore
to

to supply the poverty of common language,
he has recourse to METAPHORS and IMAGES *;
which,

---

* LONGINUS is of opinion, that the use of metaphors and figures has an admirable effect in composition, both by heightening the sublime, and giving
greater force to the pathetic; and likewise observes,
that while figures give a particular efficacy to the sublime, they receive equal benefit from it in turn:

Εγαι δε παιυ συντομον, οτι φυσει πως συμμαχει τω ύψει τα
χημαJα, και παλιν αντισυμμαχειται θαυμαςως ύπ' αυτε. De
Sublim. sect. 17.

He observes in another place, that the crowding figures
together, is a method of exciting the more violent com-
motions of the mind:

Ακρως δε και ή επι ταυτο συνοδ@. των χηματων ειωθε κινειν, οταν
δυο η τρια, οιον καJα συμμοριαν ανακιςναμινα, αλληλοις εραιζε
την ιχυν της πειθω το καλλ@. De Sublim. sect. 20.

QUINTILIAN admits of metaphors in an oration
only, in order to fill up a vacant place, or when they
have greater force than those unornamented expressions
in whose place they are substituted: " Metaphora enim
" aut vacantem occupare locum debet, aut si in alie-
" num venit, plus valere eo quod expellit." Instit.
lib. viii. cap. 6. — If however we reflect, that Poetry,
whose capital end it is to please, requires more ornament than Prose composition, in order to the attainment

which, though they may fometimes occafion
the want of precifion, will always elevate
his ftile, as well as give a peculiar dignity
and energy to his fentiments *. An original Author indeed will frequently be apt to
exceed in the ufe of this ornament, by pour-
ing forth fuch a blaze of imagery, as to
dazzle and overpower the mental fight; the
effect of which is, that his Writings become
obfcure †, if not unintelligible to common
Readers;

---

ment of that end, we fhall fee the neceffity of allowing to Poets greater licence in the ufe of metaphors and
imagery, than to any other Authors whatever.

\* " Sed illud quoque, de quo in argumentis dixi-
" mus, fimilitudinis genus ornat orationem, facitque
" fublimem, floridam, jucundam, mirabilem." *Inftit.*
lib. viii. cap. 3. — The above remark, the Reader will
obferve, is ftill more eminently true with refpect to the
influence of Imagery in Poetry.

† It is a maxim laid down by QUINTILIAN, that
in an oration the image fhould be clearer than that
which it is adduced to illuftrate: " Debet enim quod
" illuftrandæ alterius rei gratia affumitur, ipfum effo
" clarius eo quod illuminat." *Ibid.* He obferves a

Readers; juft as the eye is for fome time
rendered incapable of diftinguifhing the objects that are prefented to it, after having
ftedfaftly contemplated the Sun. Well
chofen images, happily adapted to the purpofe for which they are adduced, if not too
frequently employed, produce a fine effect
in Poetry. They impart a pleafing gratification to the mind, arifing from the difcovery of the refemblance betwixt the fimili-
tude and the object to which it is compared ;
they remarkably enliven defcription, at the
fame time that they embellifh it with additional graces * ; they give force as well as

---

little above, that one of the effential excellencies of
Imagery confifts in its being ufeful for illuftration :
" Præclare vero ad inferendam rebus lucem, repertæ
" funt fimilitudines." This likewife is one of its ufes
in Poetry.

* QUINTILIAN, fpeaking of metaphors, makes
the following obfervation concerning them : " Tum
" ita jucunda atque nitida, ut in oratione quamlibet
" clara, proprio tamen lumine eluceat. Neque enim
" vulgaris effe, nec humilis, nec infuavis, recte modo
" adfcita poteft." Inftit. lib. viii. cap. 6.

grandeur

grandeur to the ftile of Poetry, and are a
principal fource of thofe exquifite fenfations,
which it is calculated to infpire. On the
other hand, the too liberal ufe of IMAGERY
even in Poetry (befides that obfcurity which
it occafions to the ordinary clafs of Readers,
as well as that fatigue which the Imagination experiences from its exceffive glare) fo
difgufts the mind with the perpetual labour
of tracing relations and refemblances, which
cannot always be immediately perceived, that
the tide of paffion is by this means diverted,
if it doth not fubfide, and the pleafure
arifing from poetic imitation is greatly di-
minifhed, if not utterly deftroyed. A Writer
however, who is only poffeffed of a moderate
degree of Genius, is in very little hazard of
falling into this extreme. His imagination
is not extenfive enough to comprehend thofe
remote analogies which fubfift betwixt different objects in nature, nor does it poffefs
force fufficient to throw off a bold and glowing image founded upon fuch analogies: the
performances of fuch an Author therefore

L 2                    will

will either be intirely deftitute of the images
of Poetry, excepting fuch as arife from the
moft obvious relations of ideas; or elfe thofe
which he adopts will be borrowed from Authors of fuperior Genius.   Hence it is, that
the images of HOMER have been fo often
copied by modern Poets, who either pos-
feffed not fertility of Invention enough to
ftrike out new fimilitudes for themfelves, or
dared not to exert it.   A Poet endued with
a truly original Genius, will however be under no neceffity of drawing any of the materials of his compofition from the Works
of preceding Bards; fince he has an unfail-
ing refource in the exuberance of his own
Imagination, which will furnifh him with a
redundance of all thofe materials, and particularly with an inexhauftible variety of
new and fplendid imagery, which muft be
regarded as one diftinguifhing mark of original poetic Genius.

The fourth and laft fpecies of Invention,
by which we obferved this quality to be indicated,

dicated, was that of SENTIMENT. An original Genius in Poetry will ſtrike out NEW SENTIMENTS, as well as NEW IMAGES, on every ſubject on which he employs his talents; and he has the peculiar felicity of ſtriking out ſuch as are moſt proper to the ſubject and to the occaſion. An univerſal Genius is a very extraordinary phenomenon. Even a talent for acquiring excellence in the various branches of any one art, is very rarely beſtowed; ſo limited in general are the faculties of the human mind. Thus we ſeldom find a Genius for Tragedy and Comedy, or a Genius for the more ſublime ſpecies of Hiſtory-painting, and for pieces of Drollery and Humour in low life, united in the ſame perſon. We have already obſerved, in a note at the beginning of this ſection, that there are different kinds, as well as degrees of Originality; we are not therefore to expect, that an original Genius in Poetry ſhould attain eminence in every branch of his profeſſion; it is enough if he diſtinguiſh himſelf in one branch, whatever

L 3

it

it may be. What we would be underſtood
to maintain is this; that original Genius
will dictate the moſt proper ſentiments on
every ſubject, and in every ſpecies of Poetry,
INDISCRIMINATELY; but that it will dictate
the ſentiments moſt proper to that particular ſpecies to which it is ADAPTED, and to
which it applies its inventive powers. If,
for inſtance, we ſuppoſe this quality adapted
to Epic Poetry, it will diſcover itſelf in the
invention both of ſublime and pathetic ſentiments, which will at once excite aſtoniſhment, and penetrate the heart. To a perſon who poſſeſſes a talent for this higheſt
ſpecies of Poetry, ſuch ſentiments are as it
were congenial; they ariſe naturally and
ſpontaneouſly to his imagination. The
ſublime, in particular, is the proper walk
of a great Genius, in which it delights
to range, and in which alone it can diſplay its powers to advantage, or put forth
its ſtrength. As ſuch a Genius always attempts to graſp the moſt ſtupendous objects,

jects *, it is much more delighted with sur-
veying the rude magnificence of nature, than
the elegant decorations of art; since the latter produce only an agreeable sensation of
pleasure; but the former throws the soul
into a divine transport of admiration † and
amazement,

---

* LONGINUS, that admirable Critic, illustrates this
observation very beautifully:

Ενθεν φυσικως πως αγομενοι μα δι υ τα μικρα ρειθρα θαυμα-
ζομεν, ει και διαυγη και χρησμια· αλλα τον Νειλον, και Ιστρον η
Ρηνον, πολυ δ' ετι μαλλον τον Ωκεανον. Ου δι γε το υφ' ημων τυτι
φλογιον ανακαιομενον, επει καθαρον σωζει το φιγ[©], εκπληττο-
μεθα των υρανιων μαλλον, και τοι πολλακις επισκοτυμενων· υ δε
των της Αιτνης κρατηρων αξιοθαυμαστοτερον νομιζομεν, 'ης αι ανα-
χοαι πετρας τι εκ βυθυ και ολας οχθας ανωφερυσι, και ποταμυς
ενιοτε τυ γηινυ εκεινυ και αυτυ μονυ προχεωσι πυρ©. *De Sublim.* cap. 35.

† The above-mentioned excellent Author gives the
following just description of the nature, characteristics,
and effects of true sublimity:

Τυτο γαρ τω οντι μεγα, υ πολλη μεν η αναθεωρησις, δυσκολ©-
δε, μαλλον δ' αδυ ιαι[©· η κατεξαναστασις· ιχυρα δι η μνημη, και
δυσεξαλειπι[©. Ὁλως δε καλα νομιζε υψη και αληθινα, τα δια
παντ©· αρισκοντα και πασιν. *Ibid.* cap. 7.

L 4                                    The

amazement, which occupies and fills the mind, and at the fame time infpires that folemn dread, that religious awe, which naturally refults from the contemplation of the vaft and wonderful. By dwelling on fuch fubjects, the foul is elevated to a fenfe of its own dignity and greatnefs.

We obferved likewife, that an Author poffeffed of that kind and degree of original Genius which is adapted to Epic Poetry, will admirably fucceed in the invention of

---

The *Roman* Critic judicioufly obferves, that in forming our opinion of fublimity in compofition, we ought to confider the nature of the fubject on which it is employed, and how far it is fuitable to the kind of ornament made ufe of; becaufe, where the fubject itfelf is mean, fublimity degenerates into bombaft:

" Clara illa atque fublimia, plerunque materiæ modo
" cernenda funt. Quod enim alibi magnificum, tumi-
" dum alibi. Et quæ humilia circa res magnas, apta
" circa minores videntur. Et ficut in oratione nitida
" notabile eft humilius verbum, & velut macula: ita
" a fermone tenui fublime nitidumque difcordat, fitque
" corruptum, quia in plano tumet." QUINT. *Inftit.*
lib. viii. cap. 3.

PATHETIC

PATHETIC * as well as SUBLIME fentiments;
if an Author can be faid to invent fentiments which rife to the imagination, in a
manner by a fimple volition, without any
labour, and almoft without any effort.
Such a perfon being endued with a vivacity
and vigour of Imagination, as well as an
exquifite fenfibility of every emotion, whether pleafant or painful, which can affect
the human heart, has nothing elfe to do, in
order to move the paffions of others, but to
reprefent his own feelings in a ftrong and
lively manner; and to exhibit the object,
event or action he propofes to defcribe, in
that particular attitude or view, which has
moft powerfully interefted his own affec-

---

* This talent of raifing the paffions by fuitable reprefentations, feems to depend upon an extreme fenfibility both of pain and pleafure, joined to the power of
defcribing in a lively manner thofe exquifite fenfations
which we ourfelves feel.    Both the one and the other
are the infeparable concomitants of true Genius; tho'
there are many poffeffed of the former, who are not
endued with the latter.

tions,

tions, for that will moſt certainly intereſt
ours : we ſhall feel the ſame concern, and
ſhare in the ſame diſtreſs *.  Having by
this means gained an aſcendant over our
hearts, he will at pleaſure melt them into
tenderneſs and pity, or fire them with in-
dignation and rage : every paſſion will be
obedient to his impulſe, as well as ſubject
to his controul ; like the Poet deſcribed
by HORACE, he will raiſe in our ſouls

---

* ARISTOTLE obſerves, in his book on Poetry, that
there are various methods of raiſing the paſſions ; that
pity and terror may be excited by external action, particularly by the ſymptoms of diſtreſs ſtrongly impreſſed
upon the countenance ; but that a good Poet will never
have recourſe to this method as his only expedient for
moving the paſſions, but will accompliſh his end by the
very conſtitution of his fable, and the affecting nature
of the relation itſelf :

Ερι μιν υι το φοβιρον και ιλιιιον ιχ της οψιως γιιιϑαι.  Ερι
δι και ιξ αυτης της συςασιως των πραγματων, ὁπιρ ιςι προτι-
ρον και ποιητου αμιινον.  Διι γαρ και ανυ τυ ὁραν ὑτω συνιϲ-
ταναι τον μυθον ὡςι τον αχυοντα τα πραγματα γινομινα, και
φριτϊιιν και ιλιιιν ιχ των συμβαινοντων.  cap. 14.

                                                    every

every emotion of which they are fufceptible † :

*Irritat, mulcet, falfis terroribus implet*
*Ut magus, et modo me Thebis, modo ponit Athenis.*

'Tis he who gives my breaft a thoufand pains,
Can make me feel each pafsion that he feigns;
Enrage, compofe with more than magic art;
With pity and with terror tear my heart;
And fnatch me o'er the earth, or thro' the air,
To *Thebes*, to *Athens*, when he will, and where.

POPE.

The

---

† QUINTILIAN confiders the raifing the paffions of
the hearers, and carrying them along by the force of
rapid eloquence, as the higheft effort of rhetorical Genius ; and obferves, that though many of his predeceffors and cotemporaries in the rhetorical art excelled in
the argumentative part of eloquence, few had excelled
in the pathetic :

" Qui vero judicem rapere, & in quem vellet habi-
" tum animi poffet perducere, quo dicto flendum &
" irafcendum effet rarius fuit. Atque hoc eft quod
" dominatur in judiciis ; hæc eloquentiam regunt."
*Lib.* vi. *cap.* 3.

With

The fentiments of an Author of this kind *
are the natural dictates of the heart, not
fictitious or copied, but original; and it is
impoffible they fhould fail in producing
their proper effect upon the mind of the
Reader. Thefe obfervations, by which we
have endeavoured to fhew how originality
of Genius in the higher fpecies of Poetry
will difcover itfelf in the invention of fen-

---

With refpect to the higher fpecies of Poetry, Tragedy and the *Epopœa*, it is needlefs to fay how much
the pathetic ought to predominate in them; and that to
the attainment of it in an extraordinary degree, an eminent exertion of poetic Genius is effentially requifite.

* In order to intereft our affections deeply in any
caufe, and raife our paffions to the higheft degree,
LONGINUS requires that the emotion and agitation of
the Orator who addreffes us, fhould appear not to be
mechanical or premeditated, but to rife immediately
from the fubject and the occafion; in which cafe he
obferves, we fhall always feel our minds moft powerfully affected:

Αγει γαρ τα παθητικα τοτι μαλλον, οταν αυτα φαινται μη
επιτηδευειν αυτο· ὁ λιγων, αλλα γιναν ὁ καιρο·. *De Sublim.*
cap. 18.

timent,

timent, are equally applicable to its inferior fpecies; fince, as we have obferved,
original Genius will diftinguifh itfelf by the
invention of NEW fentiments on every fubject to which it applies itfelf.

Having confidered the different fpecies of
INVENTION, which appear to be characteriftical of original Genius, we fhall point out
fome other properties which indicate and
diftinguifh it.

Vivid and picturefque defcription, therefore, we confider as one of thefe. In the
fphere of Poetry, there is an infinite variety
of objects and fcenes, adapted to the different taftes of thofe who contemplate them.
A Writer however, of the kind above-mentioned, difregarding the beauties of a common landfcape, fixes his eye on thofe delightful and unfrequented retreats,which are
impervious to common view: to drop the
metaphor, out of the multiplicity of fubjects which his imagination prefents to him,
he

he felects fuch as are moft fufceptible of the
graces of poetic defcription, and adorns thefe
with all the luxuriance of an exuberant
Imagination. We fhall readily confefs, that
a talent for defcription is by no means fo
RADICAL and DISTINGUISHING a quality in
the conftitution of original Genius, as any
of the fpecies of INVENTION above-mentioned; yet this talent, when poffeffed in a
high degree, bears alfo the ftamp of originality, however the impreffion may be fomewhat fainter; and in the defcriptive pieces
of an original Author, we can trace the vivacity, the wildnefs, and the ftrength of his
Imagination. Such pieces will always be
eafily diftinguifhed from thofe of an inferior Author, which, in comparifon with
the former, will be languid, trivial, and
common.

A perfon who is deftitute of Genius, difcovers nothing new or difcriminating in the
objects which he furveys. He takes only a
general and fuperficial view of them, and

is

is incapable of difcerning thofe minute properties, or of relifhing thofe particular and
diftinguifhing beauties, which a lively Imagination, united with an exquifite Tafte,
can alone enable a man to conceive and admire. The defcriptions of fuch a perfon (if
he attempts to defcribe) muft neceffarily be
unanimated, undiftinguifhing, and uninterefting ; for as his imagination hath prefented to him no diftinct or vivid idea of
the fcenes or objects he has contemplated,
it is impoffible he fhould be able to give a
particular and picturefque reprefentation of
it to others. A Poet, on the other hand,
who is poffeffed of original Genius, feels in
the ftrongeft manner every impreffion made
upon the mind, by the influence of external
objects on the fenfes, or by reflection on
thofe ideas which are treafured up in the re-
pofitory of the memory, and is confequently
qualified to exprefs the vivacity and ftrength
of his own feelings. If we fuppofe a perfon
endued with this quality to defcribe real objects and fcenes, fuch as are either immediately

ately prefent to his fenfes, or recent in his remembrance; he will paint them in fuch vivid colours, and with fo many picturefque circumftances, as to convey the fame lively and fervid ideas to the mind of the Reader, which poffeffed and filled the imagination of the Author. If we fuppofe him to de-fcribe unreal objects or fcenes, fuch as exift not in nature, but may be fuppofed to exift, he will prefent to us a fucceffion of thefe equally various and wonderful, the mere creation of his own fancy; and by the ftrength of his reprefentation, will give to an illufion all the force and efficacy of a reality. As all his defcriptions will be vivid, fo all his fcenery will be rich and luxuriant in the higheft degree, fo as to evidence the extent, the copioufnefs, and the fertility of his ima-gination.

That vivacity of defcription, which we have obferved to be characteriftical of a great Genius, will in the writings of an ori-ginal one be of a kind peculiar and uncom-mon.

mon. Objects or events may be viewed in very different lights by different perfons, and admit of great variety in the reprefentation. In the defcriptions wherein fublimity is required, an Author of original Genius will fix on thofe circumftances that may raife our ideas of the object he endeavours to reprefent to the utmoft pitch. Thus the enraptured Prophet, in defcribing the defcent of the Almighty, is not contented with reprefenting the inhabitants of the earth as in a confternation, and the whole mafs of matter as agitated at his approach; but rifes much higher in his defcription, and gives fenfe as well as motion to the inanimate parts of the creation: *The mountains faw thee, and they trembled; the overflowing of the water paffed by.* Then follows a bold and happy profopopœia: *The Deep uttered his voice, and lift up his hands on high.* The former part of the defcription, where the Prophet makes the mountains fenfible of the approach, and tremble at the prefence of JEHOVAH, is truly fublime, as thefe effects give us a high idea

M of

of the majefty and power of the Almighty;
but the latter part of it, where he attributes
voice and action to the great Deep, is remarkably grand, and is indeed one of the
moft ftriking and daring perfonifications
that are to be met with either in the facred
or profane writings. It is by fixing on fuch
great and uncommon circumftances, that
an original Author difcovers the fublimity
of his Genius; circumftances which, at the
fame time that they fhew the immenfity of
his conceptions, raife our admiration and
aftonifhment to the higheft degree.

To the particular and effential ingredients of original Genius above enumerated,
we fhall fubjoin three others of a more general nature; which however are as characteriftical of this uncommon endowment,
and as much diftinguifh its productions, as
any of the particular properties above fpecified. Thefe are an IRREGULAR GREAT-
NESS, WILDNESS, and ENTHUSIASM of Imagination. The qualities we have juft now
mentioned

mentioned are diſtinct from each other;
but as they are nearly allied, and are commonly found together, we include them in
one claſs, conſidering them as unitedly
forming one general indication of elevated
and original Genius; though, for the ſake
of preciſion, we ſhall treat of them ſepa-
rately.

First we obſerved, that IRREGULAR
GREATNESS of Imagination was characteriſtical of ORIGINAL GENIUS. This expreſſion is a little equivocal in its ſignification, and therefore it will be neceſſary
to aſcertain the ſenſe in which we conſider it.

An IRREGULAR GREATNESS of Imagination is ſometimes ſuppoſed to imply a
mixture of great beauties and blemiſhes,
blended together in any work of Genius;
and thus we frequently apply it to the
writings of SHAKESPEAR, whoſe excellencies are as tranſcendent, as his faults are

con-

conspicuous. Without rejecting this sense
altogether, or denying that an original
Author will be diftinguifhed by his imper-
fections as well as by his excellencies, we may
obferve, that the expreffion above-mentioned
is capable of a jufter and more determinate
meaning than that juft fpecified. It may,
we think, be more properly underftood to
fignify that native grandeur of fentiment
which difclaims all reftraint, is fubject to
no certain rule, and is therefore various and
unequal. In this fenfe principally we confider the expreffion, and are under no difficulty in declaring, that an irregular greatnefs of Imagination, as thus explained, is
one remarkable criterion of exalted and
original Genius. A perfon who is poffeffed
of this quality, naturally turns his thoughts
to the contemplation of the Grand and
Wonderful, in nature or in human life, in
the visible creation, or in that of his own
fancy. Revolving thefe awful and magnificent fcenes in his mufing mind, he labours
to exprefs in his compofitions the ideas
which

which dilate and fwell his Imagination ; but
is often unfuccefsful in his efforts.    In attempting to reprefent thefe, he feels himfelf
embarraffed ; words are too weak to convey
the ardor of his fentiments, and he frequently finks under the immenfity of his
own conceptions.    Sometimes indeed he
will be happy enough to paint his very
thought, and to excite in others the very
fentiments which he himfelf feels : he will
not always however fucceed fo well, but, on
the contrary, will often labour in a fruit-
lefs attempt; whence it fhould feem, that
his compofition will  upon certain occafions
be diftinguifhed by an irregular and unequal
greatnefs.

Whether this quality is to be afcribed to
the caufe above-mentioned in particular; or
whether it is the effect of that fiery impetuofity of Imagination, which, breaking
through the legal reftraints of criticifm, or
overleaping the mounds of authority and
cuftom, fometimes lofes fight of the Juft

and Natural, while it is in purfuit of the
New and Wonderful, and, by attempting to
rife above the fphere of Humanity, tumbles
from its towering height ; or laftly, whether
it is to be ultimately derived from the unavoidable imperfection of the human faculties, which admit not of perpetual extenfion, and are apt to flag in a long, though
rapid flight ; whichfoever of thefe may be the
caufe of the phenomenon above-mentioned, or whether all of them may contribute
to produce it, certain it is, that an irregular
greatnefs of Imagination, implying unequal
and difproportioned grandeur, is always
difcernible in the compofitions of an original Genius, however elevated, and is therefore an univerfal characteriftic of fuch a
Genius *.

It

---

* LONGINUS maintains, that a high degree of fublimity is utterly inconfiftent with accuracy of imagination ; and that Authors of the moft elevated Genius,
at the fame time that they are capable of rifing to the
greateft excellencies, are likewife moft apt to commit
trivial

It deferves however to be obferved, that the imperfection here fuggefted, is a natural effect and a certain proof of an exuberant Imagination. Ordinary minds feldom rife above the dull uniform tenor of common fentiments, like thofe animals that are condemned to creep on the ground all the days of their life; but the moft law-lefs excurfions of an original Genius, like the flight of an eagle, are towering, though devious; its path, as the courfe of a co-met, is blazing, though irregular; and its

---

trivial faults, while they are aiming at diftinguifhed beauties. As this affertion is pretty nearly of the fame import with that above advanced, it may not be im-proper to confirm our fentiments by the authority of fo eminent a Critic:

Εγω δ' οιδα μεν, ως αι υπερβολαι μιγεθυς φυσει ηκιτα καθα-ραι. Το γαρ εν παντι ακριβες, κινδυν@· σμικροτητ@·· εν δε τοις μιγεθεσιν, ωσπερ εν τοις αγαν πλητοις, ειναι τι χρη και παρολι-γωρυμενον. Μη ποτε δε τυτο και αναγκαιον η, το τας μεν ταπει-ρας και μισας φυσεις, δια το μηδαμη παρακινδυνευειν, μηδε εφιεδαι των ακρων, αναμαρτητυς ως επι το πολυ και ασφαλιτερας διαμε-νειν τα δε μιγαλα επισφαλη δι αυτο γινεδαι το μιγεθ@·. *De Sublim:* fect. 33.

M 4 errors

errors and excellencies are equally inimi-
table.

We obferved that original Genius is likewife diftinguifhed by a WILDNESS of Imagination. This quality, fo clofely allied to
the former, feems alfo to proceed from the
fame caufes; and is at the fame time an infallible proof of a fertile and luxuriant
fancy. WILDNESS of imagery, fcenery and
fentiment, is the PASTIME of a playful and
fportive Imagination; it is the effect of its
exuberance. This character is formed by
an arbitrary affemblage of the moft extravagant, uncommon, and romantic ideas,
united in the moft fanciful combinations;
and is difplayed in grotefque figures, in
furprifing fentiments, in picturefque and
inchanting defcription. The quality of
which we are treating, wherever it is difcovered, will afford fuch a delicious entertainment to the mind, that it can fcarce
be ever fatisfied with a banquet fo exquifitely prepared; fatiety being prevented by
a fuc-

a succeſſion of dainties, ever various and ever new.

The laſt quality by which we affirmed original Genius to be characteriſed, was an ENTHUSIASM of Imagination *. It frequently

---

* Thoſe who have a curioſity to know the opinion of PLATO concerning the ENTHUSIASM of Poetry, may conſult his *Io*; where he expreſly aſſerts, that all true Poets are divinely inſpired by the Muſes; that they are incapable in their ſober ſenſes to compoſe good verſes; and that therefore, in order to their becoming excellent in their profeſſion, it is neceſſary they ſhould be hurried out of themſelves, and, like Bacchanals, be tranſported by a kind of divine fury. As his opinion, however, upon this point, will give a ſtrong ſanction to our ſentiments on that Enthuſiaſm of Imagination which we have obſerved to diſtinguiſh original poetic Genius, we ſhall preſent the Reader with two ſhort extracts from the above-mentioned Dialogue, very expreſſive of his idea concerning poetic Inſpiration:

Ουτω δε και η Μουσα ενθεους μεν ποιει αυτη, δια δε των ενθεων τουτων αλλων ενθουσιαζοντων, ορμαθ℗ εξαρταλαι. *Io.* p. 364.

SOCRATES (for he is the ſpeaker) adds a little after:

Λεγουσι μεν δηπουθεν προ℗ ημας οι ποιηται οτι απο κρηνων μελιρρυτων, εκ Μεσων κηπων᾽ τινων και ναπων δρεπομενοι τα μελη ημιν

quently happens, that the original meaning of a word is loft or become obfolete, and another very different one, through accident, cuftom or caprice, is ordinarily fubftituted in its place. Sometimes expreffions, which have been anciently taken in a good fenfe, are, by a ftrange perverfion of language, ufed in a bad one; and by this means they become obnoxious upon account of the ideas, which, in their common acceptation they excite. This is the cafe with the word ENTHUSIASM, which is almoft univerfally taken in a bad fenfe; and, being conceived to proceed from an overheated and diftempered imagination, is fuppofed to imply weaknefs, fuperftition, and madnefs. ENTHUSIASM, in this modern fenfe, is in no refpect a qualification of a Poet;

---

ἡμιν φιερησιν ὥσπιρ ἁι μιλιτlαι, κας αυτοι ὀντω πιτρομινοι· Και αληθη λιγουσι· κουφον γαρ χρημα. ποιητης ιςι, και πlηνον, και ιιρον. Και ὁ πρωτιρον οἱ⊙ τι ποιιιν πριν αν ινθι⊙ τι γινηται ιχι ικφρων, και ὁ ιις μηιτι ιν αυτω ιιη· ιως δ' αν τουτι ιχη το κlημα, αδυναl⊙ ποιιιν ιςιν ανθρωπ⊙, η χρησμωδιν Ibid.

in

in the ancient fenfe, which implied a kind
of divine INSPIRATION †, or an ardor of
Fancy wrought up to Tranfport, we not
only admit, but deem it an effential one.

A glowing ardor of Imagination is indeed
(if we may be permitted the expreffion) the
very foul of Poetry.    It is the principal
fource of INSPIRATION; and the Poet who
is poffeffed of it, like the *Delphian* Prieftefs,
is animated with a kind of DIVINE FURY.
The intenfenefs and vigour of his fenfations produce that ENTHUSIASM of Imagination, which as it were hurries the mind
out of itfelf; and which is vented in warm
and vehement defcription, exciting in every
fufceptible breaft the fame emotions that
were felt by the Author himfelf.    It is this
ENTHUSIASM which gives life and ftrength
to poetical reprefentations, renders them
ftriking imitations of nature, and thereby

---

† The etymology of the word ENTHUSIASM, which
is ωθιΘ, will afcertain its original fenfe.

produces that inchanting delight which genuine Poetry is calculated to infpire. Without this animating principle, all poetical and
rhetorical compofitions are fpiritlefs and
languid, like thofe bodies that are drained
of their vital juices : they are therefore
read with indifference or infipidity ; the
harmony of the numbers, if harmonious,
may tickle the ear, but being deftitute of
nerves, that is of paffion and fentiment, they
can never affect the heart.

Thus we have pointed out and illuftrated
the moft diftinguifhing ingredients of ORI-
GINAL GENIUS in Poetry ; we fhall conclude
the prefent fection with inquiring into the
firft and moft natural exertions of Genius in
this divine art.

We may venture then to lay it down as
a pofition highly probable, that the firft
effays of original Genius will be in ALLE-
GORIES, VISIONS, or the creation of ideal
beings, of one kind or another.  There is

no

no kind of Invention, in which there is fuller fcope afforded to the exercife of Imagination, than in that of ALLEGORY; which has this advantage over moft other fables, that in it the Author is by no means reftricted to fuch an exact probability, as is required in thofe fables that inftruct us by a reprefentation of actions, which, though not real, muft always however be fuch as might have happened. Let it be obferved, that we are here fpeaking of ALLEGORY in its utmoft latitude. We are not ignorant that there is a fpecies of it, which, like the Epic fable, attempts to inftruct by the invention of a feries of incidents ftrictly probable. Such are the beautiful and ftriking ALLEGORIES contained in different parts of the Sacred Writings. But there is another kind of ALLEGORICAL fable, in which there is very little regard fhewn to probability. Its object alfo is inftruction; though it does not endeavour to inftruct by real or probable actions; but wrapt in a veil of exaggerated, yet delicate and appofite fiction,

tion, is ſtudious at once to delight the
imagination, and to impreſs ſome important maxim upon the mind. Of this kind
is the *Fairy Queen* of SPENSER. As in this
ſpecies of ALLEGORY, we neither expect
what is true, nor what is like the truth; ſo
we read ſuch fabulous compoſitions, partly
for the ſake of the morals they contain,
but principally for the ſake of gratifying
that curioſity ſo deeply implanted in the
human mind, of becoming acquainted with
new and marvellous events. We are in
this caſe in a great meaſure upon our
guard againſt the deluſions of fancy; are
highly pleaſed with the narrative, though
we do not allow it to impoſe upon us ſo
far as to obtain our credit. Yet ſuch is
the power of ingenious fiction over our
minds, that we are not only captivated
and intereſted by a relation of ſurpriſing
incidents, though very improbable, but,
during the time of the relation at leaſt,
we forget that they are fictitious, and almoſt fancy them to be real. This deceit,
however,

however, lasts no longer than the perusal, in which we are too much agitated to reflect on the probability or improbability of the events related; but when that is over, the inchantment vanishes in the cool moment of deliberation; and, being left at leisure to think and reason, we never admit as true what is not strictly probable.

As we are treating of allegorical fables, it may not be amiss to observe, with regard to the kind last mentioned in particular, that the liberties indulged to it, though prodigiously various and extensive, are not however without certain restrictions. Thus, though we do not require probability in the general contexture of the fable, justness of manners must be preserved in this, as well as in the other species of fabulous composition; the incidents must be suitable to the characters to which they are accommodated; those incidents must likewise clearly point out or imply

imply the moral they are intended to illuftrate; and they muft, in order to captivate the Imagination, be new and furprifing, at the fame time that they are to
be perfectly confiftent with each other.
It is evident however, that thefe flight
reftraints prove no real impediment to the
natural impulfe and excurfions of Genius,
but that they ferve rather to point and re-
gulate its courfe. It is likewife equally
evident, that this laft mentioned fpecies
of Allegory prefents a noble field for the
difplay of a rich and luxuriant Imagination; and that to excel in it, requires the
utmoft fertility of Invention, fince every
mafterly compofition of this kind muft be
the mere creation of the Poet's fancy.

We obferved likewife, that ORIGINAL
GENIUS will naturally difcover itfelf in VI-
SIONS. This is a fpecies of fiction, to fucceed in which with applaufe, requires as
much poetic Infpiration as any other fpecies
of compofition whatever. That Enthufiafm

fiafm of Imagination, which we confidered as an effential characteriftic of original Genius, is indifpenfibly neceffary to the enraptured Bard, who would make his Readers feel thofe impetuous tranfports of paffion which occupy and actuate his own mind. He muft himfelf be wrought up to a high pitch of extafy, if he expects to throw us into it. Indeed it is the peculiar felicity of an original Author to feel in the moft exquifite degree every emotion, and to fee every fcene he defcribes. By the vigorous effort of a creative Imagination, he calls fhadowy fubftances and unreal objects into exiftence. They are prefent to his view, and glide, like fpectres, in filent, fullen majefty, before his aftonifhed and intranced fight. In reading the defcription of fuch apparitions, we partake of the Author's emotion ; the blood runs chill in our veins, and our hair ftiffens with horror.

It would far exceed the bounds prefcribed to this Effay, to point out all the particu-

N                                                    lar

lar tracks which an original Genius will ftrike out in the extenfive fphere of Imagination, as thofe paths are fo various and devious. In the mean time we may obferve, that as the hand of Nature hath ftamped different minds with a different kind and degree of Originality, giving each a particular bent to one certain objeƈt or purfuit; original Authors will purfue the track marked out by Nature, by faithfully following which they can alone hope for immortality to their writings and reputation. Thus while one Writer, obeying the impulfe of his Genius, difplays the exuberance of his Fancy in the beautiful and furprifing fiƈtions of Allegory; another difcovers the fertility and extent of his Imagination, as well as the juftnefs of his Judgment, in the conduƈt of the Epic or Dramatic Fable, in which he raifes our admiration, our terror, or our pity, as occafion may require.

Upon the whole, we need not hefitate to affirm, that original Genius will probably difcover

difcover itfelf either in ALLEGORIES, VISIONS, or in the creation of ideal figures of one kind or another. The probability that it will do fo, is derived from that innate tendency to FICTION which diftinguifhes fuch a Genius, and from the natural bias of FICTION to run in this particular channel: for the Imagination of a Poet, whofe Genius is truly Original, finding no objects in the vifible creation fufficiently marvellous and new, or which can give full fcope to the exercife of its powers, naturally burfts into the ideal world, in queft of more furprifing and wonderful fcenes, which it explores with infatiable curiofity, as well as with exquifite pleafure; and depending in its excurfion wholly on its own ftrength, its fuccefs in this province of FICTION will be proportionable to the plaftic power of which it is poffeffed. In cafe however the pofition juft advanced fhould appear problematical to fome, we fhall confirm it by arguments drawn from experience, which will ferve to fhew, that ORIGINAL POETIC

GENIUS

GENIUS hath in fact exerted its powers in the manner above specified *.

In proof of this assertion, we might adduce the whole system of heathen Mytho-

---

* LONGINUS considers the introducing visions into composition, and the supporting them with propriety, as one of the boldest efforts either of Rhetorical or Poetic Genius. He observes, that they contribute much to the grandeur, to the splendor, and to the efficacy of an oration in particular :

Ογκε και μεγαληγοριας, και αγων⊙· επι τετοις, ω νεανια, και αἱ φαντασιαι παρασκευαςικωταται· ειδωλοποιϊας αυτας ενιοι λεγουσι. Καλειται μεν γαρ κοινως φαντασια, παν εννοημα λογου γεννητικον ὁπωσεν παριςαμενον· ιδιως δ' επι τετων κεκρατηκε τουνομα, οταν ἁ λεγης, ὑπ' ενθεσιασμε και παθες βλεπειν δοκης, και ὑπ' οψιν τιθης τοις ακεουσιν. De Sublim. sect. 15.

After having given this account of the nature and effect of a vision introduced into an oration, he observes, that there is a difference betwixt visions adapted to Rhetoric, and such as are adapted to Poetry; but that they both concur in producing a violent commotion of mind :

Ὡς δ' ἑτερον τι ἡ ῥητορικη φαντασια βελεται, και ἑτερον η παρα ποιηταις, εκ αν λαθοι σε, εδ' ὁτι της μεν εν ποιησει τελ⊙· ερεν εκπληξις, της δ' εν λογοις εναργεια αμφοτεραι δ' ὁμως τετ' επιζητουσι το συγκεκινημενον. Ibid.

logy.

logy. What are all the fabulous and allegorical relations of antiquity concerning the nature, generation, powers and offices of the Pagan Deities, but the inventions of men of Genius? Poets and Priests were unquestionably the original Authors of all the Theological Systems of the Gentile world. A ray, ultimately derived from divine Revelation, did sometimes indeed burst through the cloud of human error, but was soon obscured, if not smothered, by the superstitions of men; and oral Tradition, that fallacious guide, was buried under a mass of absurdity and folly. Though the heathen Theology must be confessed to be the disgrace and degradation of human reason, yet it must also be acknowledged to be a remarkable proof of the creative power of human Imagination; and at the same time that we condemn it as a religious Creed, we must admire it as a system of ingenious Fiction. The *Greek* Theology was of all other systems the most ingenious. What a strange, but fanciful account, may we collect from

N 3 those

thofe ancient Authors, HOMER and HESIOD, of the nature and employment of the numerous Deities which *Greece* acknowledged? We find the celeftial Divinities, JUPITER and JUNO, MINERVA and VENUS, MARS and APOLLO, fometimes quaffing nectar in their golden cups, and repofing themfelves in indolent tranquillity, ferved by HEBE, and attended by MERCURY, the fwift-winged meffenger of the Gods: at other times we fee them mixing among the *Trojan* and *Grecian* hofts, taking part in mortal quarrels, as partiality or favour dictated; infpiring the army whofe caufe they embraced with their counfel, and aiding it by their power; driving on or ftemming the tide of battle, and alternately haftening and retarding the decrees of fate. CERES has the earth for her province, and is the bounteous giver of the golden grain; NEPTUNE fways the ocean with his trident; and PLUTO, feated on his throne in gloomy majefty, rules the dominions of the world below. Need we mention, as proofs of wild

and

and exuberant Fancy, the pleasures and beauties of *Elysium*, contrasted with the torments and horrors of dark *Tartarus*? Need we mention the black *Cocytus*, the flaming *Phlegethon*; the punishment of TANTALUS, the ever-rolling stone of SISYPHUS, the wheel of IXION, and the fruitless perpetual labours of the *Danaids*?

It would be impracticable, as well as tedious and unnecessary to enumerate the vast multitude of subordinate Deities which *Greece* adored. All nature was replenished with them; and each particular part had its tutelar Divinity. Thus while DIANA and her train of woodland nymphs, together with her ministers the *Dryads* and *Hamadryads*, were adored by huntsmen as the Sovereigns of the woods, PAN received the homage of the simple shepherds, was considered as the Guardian of their flocks, and the rural God who taught them to play on the oaten pipe. To these we may join the Satyrs and Fawns, the *Naiads* of the rivers

N 4 sporting

fporting on the limpid ftream, and the nymphs of the fea rifing with THETIS from their watry beds, and lightly floating on the furface of the waves; the ftory of PROME- THEUS chained to a rock, and devoured by vulturs, for ftealing fire from Heaven, to animate his workmanfhip of clay; the loves of JUPITER and LEDA; the fable of MI- NERVA's iffuing from the head of JUPITER; the wars of the latter with the Giants, and the fiction of VULCAN's being hurled from Heaven, with hideous ruin and combuftion, by the wrath of the *Olympian* King. We may farther add thofe exquifite inventions of the Mufes and Graces, of Fortune and the Fates, of Auguries and Oracles, of the fprings of *Helicon*, and infpirations of *Par- naffus*, the dreams of *Pindus* and the *Aonian* maids; the expedition of the *Argonauts*; the labours of HERCULES and of THESEUS; the fabulous, but pleafing relations of the golden age; the contention of the Goddeffes on mount *Ida*, for the prize of beauty; the admirable allegory of PRODICUS, in which

Virtue

Virtue and Pleasure are introduced as addreffing HERCULES, and the excellent allegorical picture of human life by CEBES: all
which ingenious fables confidered together,
and many more of them that might be mentioned, are ftriking indications of the plaftic
power of the human mind, and undeniable
proofs of true Genius in the original In-
venters.

From this general and imperfect view of
the *Greek* Mythology, it is evident, that
original Genius did in ancient *Greece* always
difcover itfelf in allegorical Fiction, or in
the creation of ideal figures of one kind or
another; in inventing and adding new fables to the received fyftem of Mythology, or
in altering and improving thofe that had
been already invented. The immenfe and
multifarious fyftem of the *Greek* Theology
was a work of many centuries, and rofe
gradually to that height in which it now
appears. Some additions were daily made
to it by the Poets and men of lively Imagination,

nation, till that huge pile of Superſtition was completed, which, in its ruins, exhibits ſo ſtriking a monument of human ingenuity and folly.    If, after what has been alledged, any one ſhould queſtion whether the fabulous Theology now conſidered, be an effect or indication of ORIGINAL GENIUS, we would only deſire him to ſuppoſe the Mythology of HOMER annihilated.    What a blank would ſuch annihilation make in the divine *Iliad!* Deſtitute of its celeſtial machinery, would it not be in a great meaſure an inanimate maſs? It would at leaſt loſe much of that variety, dignity and grandeur, which we admire in it at preſent, and much of that pleaſing and ſurpriſing fiction, which gives ſuch exquiſite delight to the Imagination.

It would be eaſy to confirm the poſition we have laid down, that ORIGINAL GENIUS always diſcovers itſelf in Allegories, Viſions, or the invention of ideal Characters, by examples drawn from the Eaſtern and the

*Egyptian*

*Egyptian* Mythology, which was so full of Fable and hieroglyphical Emblems; but we shall wave the consideration of these as superfluous, after what hath been already urged, and conclude this part of our subject with observing, that the Eastern manner of writing is, and hath ever been characterised by a remarkable boldness of sentiment and expression, by the most rhetorical and poetical figures of speech; and that many of the compositions of the Eastern nations abound with Allegories, Visions and Dreams; of which we have several admirable examples in the sacred Writings.

SECTION

# SECTION IV.

## OF

## ORIGINAL

## GENIUS

### IN THE OTHER

## FINE ARTS.

THOUGH it is Poetry that affords the ampleſt ſcope for the exertion of the powers of Imagination, and for the moſt advantageous diſplay of ORIGINAL GENIUS; yet a very high degree of this quality may be diſcovered in ſome of the other fine Arts, and a greater or leſs degree of it in all of them; as they are all indebted, though not equally, to that faculty by which we

have

have ſhewn true Genius to be principally conſtituted.

Having conſidered the exertions of ORI-GINAL GENIUS in Poetry at great length in the preceding ſection, which indeed was the principal intention of this Eſſay, we ſhall in the preſent ſection, in order to render the deſign more complete, point out, though with greater brevity, the efforts of GENIUS in the other liberal Arts, and en-deavour to aſcertain the degree in which it will exert itſelf in each of them.  Of theſe the art of Painting claims our firſt attention.

To an eminence in certain branches of this art, the greateſt ſhare of Imagination, next to what is required in Poetry, ſeems to be eſſentially neceſſary.  Other branches however there are, in which a much leſs proportion of this talent is requiſite, and in which indeed ORIGINAL GENIUS cannot be diſplayed.  We omit, as foreign to our pur-poſe, pofe, the confideration of thefe inferior departments in the art of Painting, though fuccefsful attempts in them may indicate a great deal of ingenuity and fkill; regarding only thofe higher claffes, in which ORICINAL GENIUS may exert itfelf to advantage.

We may obferve in general, that as the power of INVENTION is the diftinguifhing ingredient of ORIGINAL GENIUS in all the fine Arts, as well as in Science; fo, in whatever degree INVENTION is difplayed in either of thefe, in the fame degree ORIGINALITY of Genius will always be difcovered. This diftinction will exclude all PORTRAITS in Painting, however excellent, and many DESCRIPTIVE PIECES in Poetry, though copied from nature, from any pretenfions to ORIGINALITY, ftrictly confidered. Both may difcover great vivacity and ftrength of Imagination; but as there is no fiction, nothing invented in either, they can only be regarded at beft as the firft and moft

complete

complete COPIES of the true ORIGINALS. In common language indeed we talk of ORIGINAL portraits, by which we mean pictures drawn from the life. The propriety of this epithet we shall not dispute. Such pictures are unquestionably in one sense ORIGINAL, as they are the first draughts, of which the succeeding ones are but COPIES. In strictness of speech however, such draughts themselves are only the COPIES or RESEMBLANCES of Nature, to execute which does not require INVENTION, and consequently does not indicate or presuppose ORIGINALITY of Genius. We must therefore have recourse to some higher branch of the art we are treating of, where this talent may be displayed to advantage, and that branch is HISTORY-PAINTING.

The History Painter *, as well as the
Epic

---

* As Poetry and Painting are in most respects similar, it will be no incurious inquiry to examine into
the

Epic Poet, commonly takes the subject
of

---

the degree of Imagination requisite to form an eminent
Painter, compared with that which is necessary to form
a great Poet.   Every one who is in any measure acquainted with the respective natures of the above-mentioned arts, must observe a very close affinity betwixt
them, and that to excel in either of them a very high
degree of Imagination is indispensibly required.   An
accurate observer however will discover the different
proportions of this quality that are appropriated and
requisite to each.   Having one common end in view,
the representation of human characters, passions and
events, or the representation of those objects which
are either presented to the senses, or are the creation
of fancy, he will perceive that they both accomplish
this end by IMITATION, though by a different kind
of it.   The Poet represents the objects of which he intends to give us an idea, by lively and affecting de-
scription, so as to make us in a manner see every thing
he describes.   The Painter exhibits the representation
of these objects to us upon canvas ; and, by the happy
union of light and shade, and the strange illusion of
colours, deceives us almost into a belief of the reality
of their existence.   Both artists must have their imaginations impressed with a very vivid idea of the objects
they intend to represent, and this idea must fill and
occupy their minds ; but a greater compass of Fancy is
required in the Poet than in the Painter ; because a
greater variety of ideas must necessarily pass in succes-
sion

of his piece from an authentic or traditionary

---

fion through his mind, which he muſt aſſociate, compound and disjoin, as occaſion may require. A multitude of fleeting objeĉts glide before his imagination at
once, of which he muſt catch the evaneſcent forms:
he muſt at the ſame time comprehend theſe in one inſtantaneous glance of thought, and delineate them as
they riſe and diſappear, in ſuch a manner as to give
them a kind of ſtability in deſcription. While the
fertility and extent of the Poet's fancy is diſcovered by
the croud of ideas which pour In upon his mind from
all quarters, and which he raiſes by a ſort of magical
inchantment, he has likewiſe occaſion for the niceſt
Judgment in ſeleĉting, combining and arranging theſe
ideas in their proper claſſes. Being obliged to deſcribe
objeĉts and events, not only as they appear to a ſuperficial obſerver, but with all thoſe concomitant circum-
ſtances which eſcape common notice, and in connection with their cauſes and conſequences, he is under a
neceſſity of employing the utmoſt extent of Imagination in repreſenting the former, and the utmoſt acute-
neſs of the reaſoning faculty in tracing the latter.

On the other hand, the whole attention of the
Painter is ingroſſed by that ſingle idea, whatever it
may be, which he intends to expreſs in his piĉture.
It is true, a piece of hiſtory-painting admits of great
variety in the attitude, air, features and paſſions of the
different figures which compoſe it; and conſequently,

O                    INVEN-

ary relation of some important event, which
forms

---

INVENTION and DESIGN; the former of which comprehends the general disposition of the work, and the
whole symmetry of it taken together, the latter the
particular posture of the several figures, and their different characters as distinguished from each other by
their corresponding signatures in the countenance, will
require a considerable compass of Imagination ; because
the Painter, before he begins to work on his piece,
must include these circumstances in one general idea,
and give proper attention to them in his progress : but
while he is employed in a particular department of the
work, in expressing the peculiar character or passion of
any individual figure, he collects his attention, fixes it
on a single point, on the image which is present to his
mind ; and he delineates upon the cloth the very transcript of his thought. Thus he proceeds gradually, in
expressing one idea after another, till he has finished
his piece; to execute which requires indeed a vivid and
vigorous Imagination, but not so extensive a one as is
necessary to form an excellent Poet.

With regard to the respective effects of Poetry and
Painting, it must be confessed, that the art of the
Painter generally produces the greatest and most agreeable deception ; as the materials he employs contribute
to the fallacy of the senses, and are admirably calculated to assist the Imagination in imposing upon itself.
Hence the pleasure we derive from the view of a fine
picture

forms the groundwork of the picture, as it
does

---

picture is immediate ; while the fubfequent fatisfaction
which we feel, in difcovering the juftnefs of the imitation, and its refemblance to the original, increafes that
pleafure.

To compenfate this advantage however, which Painting has over her fifter art, Poetry may boaft another,
in which the former muft yield the preeminence.  If
the Painter has the happinefs to exhibit a ftronger
likenefs in thofe features he endeavours to exprefs, the
Poet prefents us with a more complete refemblance of
the whole figure taken together ; for in many cafes,
words may defcribe what colours cannot paint.  We
fhall illuftrate this obfervation by an example : Suppofe
a Painter was defired to reprefent upon canvas the celebrated Interview between ALEXANDER and the Mo-
ther and Queen of DARIUS, after the battle of *Iffus*.
In fuch a draught he would temper the fiercenefs of
the Conqueror with the generous humanity of the
Hero, who fympathifes with the miferies of the unfortunate.  In the countenances of the forrowful Queens
would appear that dignity of diftrefs which was fuitable to their fituation, and that profound refpect which
the prefence of their royal vifitant was calculated to
infpire.  But hiftory informs us, that after mutual
compliments were over, ALEXANDER difcovered fo
much generofity, mildnefs, and compaffion in his be-
haviour to them, as to conciliate their efteem and con-

fidence,

does of the poem. The fuperftructure however

―――――――――――――――

fidence, as well as to excite their admiration and gratitude. Thefe unexpected offices of kindnefs could not
fail to diffufe that joy over the countenance, which is
the effect of a pleafing furprife, and which confequently
ought to have been expreffed by the Artift, had it been
practicable to blend the air of refpectful humility and
dejected melancholy, with that of unfufpecting confi-
dence and undiffembled gratitude. That this could
not be done, muft be imputed, not to the fault of the
Painter, but to the imperfection of his art; or rather,
to an impoffibility in the nature of the thing, of giving different and oppofite expreffions to the countenances of the fame perfons in the fame picture. To
do this, the Painter muft give us two diftinct pictures;
whereas the Poet can, in one and the fame relation,
give us a lively idea of all the different emotions of the
human heart; or rather can make us feel thofe emotions he fo pathetically defcribes. We may farther
obferve, that in order to form a proper notion of a
piece of HISTORY PAINTING, it is neceffary we fhould
not only be well acquainted with thofe hiftorical trans-
actions which the ingenious Artift intends, by the moft
ftriking reprefentation, to recal to our remembrance;
but we muft likewife keep in mind the precife inftant
of time when they are fuppofed to have happened;
becaufe by not knowing, or not attending to this circumftance, the beauty and emphafis of the execution
is intirely loft to us.

We

ever muſt in both caſes be the work of
thoſe

---

We ſhall conclude this note, which we are afraid is
already ſwelled to too great a length, with remarking,
that every poſſible event, with every poſſible circum-
ſtance, may be deſcribed by language, though they
cannot be delineated by colours.    Let us alſo illuſtrate
this remark by an example : Imagine a Painter ſet to
work on a deſcriptive piece, that, for inſtance, of a
Storm at Sea.    In order to give us a ſuitable idea of
this dreadful ſcene, he paints the foming billows daſh-
ing againſt the ſides of the veſſel, ſome of them over-
whelming her, while ſhe is juſt ready to burſt aſunder
with the impetuous ſhock of conflicting elements. We
ſee her ſtripped of her rigging, her maſts broken, the
ſhip herſelf laid almoſt on her ſide, by the violence of
the tempeſt ; and we perceive terror, amazement and
deſpair, impreſſed on the ghaſtly countenances of the
diſtracted mariners.    Even thus far the repreſentation
is lively ; but the Poet goes farther.    He introduces
ſome great and uncommon incidents, which heighten
the horrors of the ſcene, and which the ableſt Painter,
from the unavoidable defect of his art, can never exhibit.    He makes the lightening flaſh, and the thunder
rore.    He repreſents the tottering bark, at one time
as raiſed by the billows to the clouds, at another as
plunged into the unfathomable depths of the ocean ;
while, to complete the diſmal and terrific ſcene, he
deſcribes the piercing ſhrieks and dying mones of the
deſpairing ſailors.    If any one ſhould queſtion the ſu-

O 3                              periority

thofe ingenious Artifts themfelves. In the
defign and ordonnance of the one, and in
the contrivance of incidents and exhibition
of charaĉters in the other, great fcope is
afforded for the exercife of the inventive
faculty. Much is to be imagined, and
much to be defcribed. In order to obtain
a clear idea of the greatnefs and originality
of Genius requifite to finifh a piece of history-painting with reputation, it will be
neceffary to recur to an example. Let us
fuppofe a man of elevated Genius in this
profeffion, employing his pencil on the celebrated fubjeĉt of PAUL preaching at *Athens*,
which has immortalifed the fame of RA-
PHAEL. Inftcad of copying after this ad-

---

periority of Poetry over Painting, at leaft in defcriptive pieces, in which indeed its fuperiority is chiefly
manifefted, let him read the defcription of a ftorm in
the firft book of the *Æneid*, or in a poem, intitled,
*The Shipwreck*, compared with fea-pieces of this kind,
drawn by the ableft Mafters in the art of Painting, and he will perhaps find reafon to difmifs his
doubts.

mired

mired Artift, we fuppofe him to fketch out
and execute the whole piece by the mere
ftrength and fertility of his own imagination, taking the groundwork only from the
facred Writings. The account which the
infpired Writer gives, though comprehenfive, is but fhort; the Painter muft imagine
the reft. He would no doubt reprefent the
eloquent Apoftle as ftanding on the fummit
of *Mars* hill, in an erect pofture, with his
hands extended, and his countenance im-
preffed with a folemn earneftnefs and ardent zeal, convincing the *Athenians* of their
fuperftition, adjuring them to renounce it,
and to believe in thofe divine doctrines, and
practife thofe excellent precepts, which, by
the authority and in the name of his Mafter, he delivered to them. The air and
attitude of this affecting Preacher would be
awful, energetic and divine: they would
be greatly venerable, yet ftrongly perfuafive. On the other hand, the audience
would appear affected in the moft different
ways imaginable. In the countenances of

O 4 many

many of them, we fhould difcover a fixed
and thoughtful attention ; in thofe of a
few others, notwithftanding the eloquence
of the Sermon, that levity and curiofity,
which were fo characteriftical of the *Athenian* people.   In the countenances of fome,
we fhould difcern the fcornful fneer of
contempt, or the fupercilious frown of dis-
dain ; while a confiderable number of them
would exhibit in their ghaftly vifages terror, confufion and anguifh, the evident
marks of convicted and felf-condemning
guilt.   We fhould diftinguifh in fome the
confirmed obftinacy of infidelity ; in others,
the hefitating fufpenfe of doubt ; in others,
the yielding compliance of affent ; in others,
the fpirited ardor of hope ; in others, the
elevated joy of exultation.

From the invention of fuch a group of
figures, and fuch a diverfity of characters ;
from the happy expreffion of fo great a variety of oppofite paffions ; we infer the vivacity, the ftrength, the originality, and
the

the extent of the Artist's Genius. To express any one passion justly, is a certain
proof that he is possessed of a lively Imagination; but to be able to express such a
number of contrary ones, all of which have
been conceived by the creative power of his
own fancy, is an infallible indication of a
Genius truly COMPREHENSIVE and ORIGI-
NAL. In such an attempt, the Artist must
draw all his stores from himself; he must
invent the figures which compose the picture; design their different attitudes; and
express the variety of passions discernible
in them, with justness and force. By ac-
complishing these purposes, the illusion is
rendered complete. Every figure in the
piece is animated with nature, and flushed
with life; and the whole painting, taken
together, at once delights the imagination,
and speaks to the heart †.

We

---

† That excellent Critic, whom we have had such
frequent occasion to quote, seems to think, that, in
some

We ſhall only farther obſerve on this
ſubjeƈt, that though ORIGINAL GENIUS is
diſplayed in the higheſt degree and in the
nobleſt ſphere in HISTORY-PAINTING, yet
it may ſometimes be diſcovered, in no inconſiderable meaſure, in DESCRIPTIVE
PIECES; at leaſt where the ingenious Artiſt,
inſtead of copying real objeƈts, exhibits, as
in the former caſe, ſuch as are the mere
creation of his own fancy. Even Land-
ſcapes, Groteſques, and pieces of ſtill Life,
when they are invented by this plaſtic power
of the mind, and not imitated from ſcenes
that aƈtually exiſt, indicate an originality

---

ſome caſes, a good piƈture may produce a ſtronger ef-
feƈt upon the mind of the ſpeƈtator, than a good oration upon the mind of the hearer. Speaking of the
efficacy of geſture and aƈtion, he obſerves;

" Nec mirum ſi iſta, quæ tamen in aliquo ſunt po-
" ſita motu, tantum in animis valent; quum piƈtura,
" tacens opus & habitus ſemper ejuſdem, ſic in in-
" timos penetret affeƈtus, ut ipſam vim dicendi non-
" nunquam ſuperare videatur." QUINTIL. Inſtit.
lib. ii. cap. 3.

of

of Genius fuitable to the objects on which
it is employed.

Thus we have feen what thofe branches
in the art of Painting are, in which original Genius will difcover itfelf; and how,
and in what degree, it will exert itfelf in
thofe branches. Let us next confider how
far this fingular talent may be difplayed in
the art of Eloquence, and what its efforts
will probably be in that art.

ARISTOTLE, that acute Philofopher as
well as judicious Critic, hath defined RHE-
TORIC to be the power of difcovering in
every fubject the topics moft fuitably adapted to the purpofes of perfuafion *. This
definition appears to be juft in general, as
it includes the principal object of Eloquence, which is doubtlefs to perfuade, by

---

* Εϛω δε η ρητορικη δυναμις περι ικαϛον τε θεωρησαι το ενδε
χομενον πιθανον. ARISTOT. lib. i. cap. 2.

convincing

convincing the judgment, and influencing the paffions. To attain this object, a variety of qualifications, rarely united in one perfon, are requifite. An extenfive and exuberant imagination, a penetrating judgment, an intimate acquaintance with human nature, with the various tempers and paffions of mankind *, and their various operations, muft concur to form the accomplifhed Orator †. Befides thefe fundamental qualifications, an exquifite fenfibility of paffion, an ardent, impetuous, and

---

* " Quis enim nefcit maximam vim exiftere Orato-
" ris in hominum mentibus, vel ad iram, aut ad odium,
" aut dolorem incitandis, vel ab hifce iifdem permoti-
" onibus ad lenitatem, mifericordiamque revocandis ?
" quæ nifi qui naturas hominum, vimque omnem hu-
" manitatis, caufasque eas, quibus mentes aut incitan-
" tur, aut reflectuntur, penitus perfpexerit; dicendo,
" quod volet, perficere non poterit." CICERO de
Oratore, lib. i. cap. 12.

† Thofe who are defirous to know the various qualifications requifite to form a complete Orator, may confult the fifth chapter of the firft book of CICERO de Oratore.

overpowering

overpowering enthufiafm of imagination,
are effentially requifite to a maftery and
fuccefs in the rhetorical art, and particularly diftinguifh an ORIGINAL GENIUS in
that profeffion †. By poffeffing the firft of
thefe qualities, the Orator is enabled to feel
every fentiment which he utters, and participate every emotion which he defcribes.
By poffeffing the laft, in conjunction with
the other, he is enabled, by a torrent of
rapid eloquence, to convey to the hearts
of his hearers, thofe ftrong and enthufi-
aftic feelings, by which he is himfelf actuated.

---

† CICERO, confidering the caufes why fo few eminent Orators have appeared in any age or country,
accounts for the fact from the inconceivable difficulty
of attaining diftinguifhed excellence in Eloquence:

" Quis enim aliud in maxima difcentium multitu-
" dine, fumma magiftrorum copia, præftantiffimis
" hominum ingeniis, infinita caufarum varietate, am-
" pliffimis Eloquentiæ propofitis præmiis, effe caufæ
" putet, nifi rei quandam incredibilem magnitudinem,
" ac difficultatem ?" De Oratore, lib. i. cap. 5.

We

We may farther obferve, that a perfon endued with an ORIGINAL GENIUS for Eloquence, will at one glance, by a kind of intuition, diftinguifh and felect the moft proper, as well as moft powerful topics of perfuafion on every fubject, and will urge them with irrefiftible energy. Thefe topics will, for the moft part, be very extraordinary, and altogether unexpected; but they will conftantly produce the intended effect. They will operate upon the mind by furprife; they will ftrike like lightening, and penetrate the heart at once.

We fhall produce a few inftances of this impaffioned and perfuafive Eloquence, from thofe illuftrious ancient Orators, DEMOSTHENES and CICERO, in order to exemplify the above remarks; and fhall tranflate the paffages for the fake of the *English* Reader. The following paffage is taken from that celebrated oration of DEMOSTHENES, which procured the banifhment of ÆSCHINES,

ÆSCHINES, his enemy and rival †. CTE-
SIPHON having propofed that a Crown of
Gold fhould be prefented to DEMOSTHE-
NES, as a teftimony of the refpect of his
fellow-citizens, upon account of the eminent fervices he had done to his country;
ÆSCHINES ftrenuoufly oppofed the motion,
as contrary to the laws; and ventured to
arraign his rival before the *Athenian* people,
accufing him of mifconduct in the courfe
of his miniftry, and charging him with
being the author of all the calamities
brought upon the *Athenians* by their war
with PHILIP. DEMOSTHENES, having vindicated his character in general from the
unjuft afperfions thrown upon it by ÆSCHI-
NES, proceeds to juftify the particular meafures which he had concerted, with the
approbation of other leading men in the
adminiftration, notwithftanding the event
of thofe meafures had been unfuccefsful.

---

† Vide DEMOSTH. *de Corona*.

Thus

Thus he introduces his ſpirited argumentation *.

This

---

* Επειδη δε πολυς τοις συμβεβηκοσιν εγκειται βουλομαι τι
και παραδοξον ειπειν· και μη προ Διος και θεων, μηδεις την
υπερβολην θαυμαση, αλλα μετ' ευνοιας ο λιγω θεωρησατω. Ει
γαρ ην απασι προδηλα τα μελλοντα γενησεσθαι, και προηδεσαν
παντες, και συ προελεγες Αισχινη, και διαμαρτυρω βοων και
κεκραγως ος ουδ' εφθεγξω, ουδ' ουτως αποστατεον τη πολει τουτων
ην, ειπερ η δοξης, η προγονων, η τε μελλοντG αιωνG ειχε λο-
γον. Νυν μεν γαρ αποτυχειν δοκει των πραγματων, ο πασι κοινον
εστιν ανθρωποις, οταν το θεω ταυτα δοκη. Τοτε δ' αξιωσα προισ-
ταται των αλλων, ειτα αποστασα τουτου, Φιλιππω προδεδωκιναι
πανίας, αν ειχεν αιτιαν. Ει γαρ ταυτα προειτο ακοντι περι ων
ουδενα κινδυνον οντινο υν εχ υπεμειναν οι προγονοι, τις ουχι κα-
τεπτυσεν αν σου. Μη γαρ της πολεως γι, μηδ' εμου. Τοισι δ' οφ-
θαλμοις, προ ΔιG, ιωρωμεν αν τους εις την πολιν ανθρωπους αφικ-
νουμενους, ει τα μεν πραγματα εις οπερ νυνι περιεστη, ηγεμων και
κυριG ηρειθη ΦιλιππG απαντων, τον δε υπερ του μη γενεσθαι ταυτα
αγωνα, ετεροι χωρις ημων, ησαν πεποιημενοι. Και ταυτα μηδε
πω ποτε της πολεως, εν τοις εμπροσθεν χρονοις ασφαλειαν αδοξον
μαλλον, η τον υπερ των καλων κινδυνον ηρημενης.

---

" But ſince my adverſary lays ſo much ſtreſs upon
events, I will venture to advance a paradox; and in
the name of JUPITER and all the Gods, let none of
you wonder at the apparent hyperbole, but let every
one attend with candour to what I am going to ſay.
If the things which afterwards happened had been ma-
nifeſt

This great Orator having by the above,
and

---

nifeſt to all, and all had foreſeen them; if even you,
Æschines, had foretold and declared them with your
bawling and thundering voice, who by the way never
till now uttered a word concerning them; even in that
caſe *Athens* ought by no means to have altered its mea-
ſures, if it had any regard to its own glory, to the
glory of its anceſtors, or to that of ſucceeding gene-
rations.   At preſent indeed it ſeems to have fallen
from its priſtine grandeur; a misfortune common to all
ſtates and all men, whenever the Deity is pleaſed to
order it ſo.   But *Athens*, having once been thought
worthy of the precedence of all the other *Grecian* Re-
publics, could not relinquiſh this glorious claim, nor
plead an exemption from the dangers attending it,
without incurring the blame and diſgrace of abandon-
ing the common intereſt to the rapacious ambition of
Philip.   If it had relinquiſhed, without a ſtruggle,
thoſe privileges which our anceſtors braved every danger to maintain, who, Æschines, would not have
deſpiſed your timid prudence? for no ſhare of the
blame could juſtly have fallen on the other members
of the commonwealth, or upon me. — Great God!
with what eyes ſhould we in that caſe have looked
upon this great multitude, aſſembled from all parts of
*Greece*, now hearing me, if things had come, by our
own faults, to the condition we ſee them in at preſent; and Philip had been created Generaliſſimo and
Sovereign of all the *Greeks*, without our having united

P                    our

and many other ftriking arguments, evinced
the rectitude of his own conduct, as well
as of the conduct of his partners in the
adminiftration, in carrying on the war
againft PHILIP, comes next to touch upon
the battle of *Chæronea*, which had been fo
fatal to the *Athenians*; and as the defeat
they had there fuftained was fuppofed to be
a confequence of the meafures that had
been adopted, this defeat was, by his ene-
mies particularly, charged upon DEMOST-
HENES, as having been the principal author
of the meafures which brought on that unhappy event. The vindication of himfelf
and his fellow-citizens, who had been either the advifers or fharers of that unfortunate, but glorious engagement, by the following aftonifhing and fublime Oath, is

---

our aid, with that of the other *Grecian* States, in
order to prevent fo great an indignity? efpecially when
we confider, that in former times it hath been always
the character of the *Athenian* Republic to prefer glorious
danger to difhonourable fafety."

one

one of the boldeſt flights of rhetorical
Genius †.

This is one of thoſe ſtrokes of Eloquence, which produce the intended effect by an inſtantaneous and irreſiſtible
impulſe, whirling away the ſouls of the

---

† Αλλ ακ εςιν ακ εςιν οπως ημαρτετε ανδρες αθηναιοι, τον
υπερ της απαντων ελευθεριας και σωτηριας, κινδυνον αραμενοι.
Ου μα τους εν μαραθωνι προκινδυνευσαντας των προγονων, και
τας εν πλαταιαις παραταξαμινας, και τας εν σαλαμινι. ναυμα-
χησαντας, και τας επ αρτεμισιω, και πολλας ετερας τας εν τοις
δημοσιοις μνημασι κειμινας αγαθας ανδρας. Ους απαντα; ομοιως
η πολις της αυτης αξιωσασα τιμης εθαψεν αιχινη.

— " But it cannot be, *Athenians*, it cannot be, that
you have erred in expoſing your lives for the freedom
and ſafety of *Greece.* — No, you have not erred, I
ſwear by your illuſtrious anceſtors, who hazarded their
lives in ſupport of the ſame glorious cauſe in the fields
of *Marathon,* by thoſe who made ſo brave a ſtand at
*Platæa,* by thoſe who fought in the ſea-engagement at
*Salamin,* by thoſe who fell at *Artemiſium,* and laſtly by
thoſe many other excellent ſoldiers and citizens, the
martyrs of liberty, who lie interred in public monuments, which this city, regarding them as worthy
of ſuch an honour, hath raiſed to their memory and
fame."

P 2                    hearers

hearers at once, without leaving them time to weigh the motives of conviction or per-suasion *.

The

---

* An Orator of common Genius would never have thought of so extraordinary a method of argumentation, as DEMOSTHENES here uses, for vindicating the conduct of the *Athenians* in hazarding the battle of *Chæronea*, and for reconciling them to the loss of it. He would probably have satisfied himself with producing precedents of the same kind, and with observing that their ancestors had fought the battles of *Marathon, Platæa, Salamin* and *Artemisium*, in defence of the liberties of *Greece*; but the *Athenian* Orator, instead of this cool reasoning, hurried away by the enthusiasm and impetuosity of his own Genius, sets before their eyes, as it were by the most sublime and striking figure, the awful shades of their fathers, who had sacrificed their lives in the cause of Liberty. By swearing by those illustrious Heroes, he raises them above the condition of humanity, and proposes them both as the objects of admiration and imitation. Nothing indeed could have been more happily calculated for comforting the *Athenians* under the defeat they had sustained at *Chæronea*, and raising their dejected spirits, than this solemn appeal to their ancestors, by which the Orator seems to put that defeat on a level with the victories

The laſt quotation we ſhall produce, from the Orations of DEMOSTHENES, ſhall be taken from his firſt *Philippic*. The Orator, having inveighed againſt the indolence of the *Athenians* in ſuffering PHILIP to

---

victories which they had obtained at *Marathon, Platæa, Salamin,* and *Artemiſium.*

Thoſe who are deſirous of ſeeing the above celebrated paſſage illuſtrated in the trueſt taſte of Criticiſm, may conſult the ſixteenth chapter of LONGINUS's Treatiſe on the *Sublime*; where that excellent Judge of the beauties of Compoſition hath obſerved, that by this ſingle figure, which he calls an Apoſtrophe, the Orator hath enrolled thoſe ancient Heroes among the Gods, and taught us that it is proper to ſwear by ſuch as die in the ſame manner :

Φαινεται δι᾽ ἑνὸς τȣ ομοτικȣ σχημαlꙩ ὁπερ ενθαδε αποϛροφην εγω καλῶ τȣς μεν προγονȣς αποθεωσας, ὁτι δει τȣς αποθανοντας ὡς θεȣς ομνυναι παριϛαιων.

From this ſhort ſpecimen, our Readers will perceive that the Critic in his illuſtration rivals the ſublimity of the Orator. For farther ſatisfaction we muſt refer them to the above-mentioned chapter, the limits of our plan not allowing us to ſwell out the page with quotations.

extend

extend his conquefts without moleftation,
addreffes them in the following clofe, pointed and energetic interrogatories, fo worthy
of the Orator and the Patriot *.

The

---

* Ποτ᾽ ꭱꭱꭱ ανδρες αθηναιοι, ποτε ἃ χρη πραξιτε. Επειδαν
τι γενηται? επιδαν τη δια αναʃκητις η? νυν δε τι χρη τα γιγνο-
μενα ηγειʃθαι? εγωμιν γαρ οιμαι τοις ελευθεροις μεγιϛην αναʃκην
την ὑπερ των πραγματων αι χυνην ειναι. Η βυλιϛθι ειπε μοι
περιοντες αυτων συνθανεϛθαι κατα την αγοραν, λεγεται τι καινον? γινοιτο γαρ αν τι καινοτερον, η μακιδων ανηρ αθηναιης κα-
ταπολιμων, και τα των ἑλληνων διοικων? ϛεθνηκε φιλιππ⊙? 
ου μα δι, αλλ αϛϑενει. Τι δυμιν διαφιρει? και γαρ αν ουτ⊙
τι παθη ταχιως υμεις ετερον φιλιππον ποιησετε, αν περι συ-
τω προσιχητι τοις πραʃμασι τον νουν ꭱδε γαρ ουτ⊙ παρα την
ꭱαυτꭱ ρωμην τοσꭱτον επευξιται οσον παρα την ημετεραν αμε-
λειαν.

" When, *Athenians,* when will you act as you
ought? When fhall fome extraordinary event roufe
you? When fhall fome imminent neceffity compel
you? But what fhall we think of the prefent juncture,
and of the events which have already happened? For
my part, I look upon the difgracefulnefs of our paft
conduct, to be the ftrongeft incentive, the moft urgent
neceffity to free men to alter their meafures, and act a
more fpirited part. Or tell me, Do you rather incline,
according to your ufual cuftom, to fanter about idle,
afking each other in the forum, What news? Can there
be

The *Athenian* Orator paints the idle curiofity of his countrymen with great mastery in the above fhort queftion, λεγεται τι
καινον? " What news?" and the eloquent
Apoftle of the Gentiles confirms this character of the *Athenians*, by the obfervation
which he made on their conduct during his
abode among them. He tells us, that
" they fpent their time wholly in hearing
" and relating fome new thing." Αθηναιοι δε
παντες εις ουδεν ετερον ευκαιρουν η λεγειν τι και ακυειν
καινοτερον *. The interrogation of the Orator, γενοιτο γαρ αν τι καινοτερον η μακεδων ανηρ,

---

be any thing more *new*, than that a man of *Macedonia* has dared to make war on the *Athenians*, and governs the reft of *Greece*? Is PHILIP dead? fays one:
No, replies another, but he is certainly fick. What,
pray, does either fignify to you? For whatever be his
cafe, whether he be fick or dead, you will foon raife
up another PHILIP, while you manage your affairs in
fo liftlefs and indolent a manner; for he hath attained
his prefent grandeur, more through your inactivity
than his own bravery."

† Acts xvii. 21.

P 4

αθηναιος

αθεναίες καταπολεμαν και το των ἑλληνων διοικων?
"Can there be any thing more new, than
that a man of *Macedonia* makes war upon
the *Athenians*, and governs the reſt of *Greece?*"
is highly ſpirited and poignant; ſhews the
diſdain with which DEMOSTHENES himſelf
viewed the inſolence of PHILIP; and was
admirably calculated to produce a ſenſe of
honeſt ſhame in the minds of his countrymen, to rouſe their ancient ſpirit of liberty,
and excite the ſtrongeſt jealouſy of the de-
ſigns of the *Macedonian* Monarch.   The art
and addreſs of the Orator is in theſe re-
ſpeᘔs truly admirable.   Every one muſt
perceive the keen and exquiſitely fine irony
of the following queſtion, Τεθνηκε φιλιππος?
"Is PHILIP dead?" and of the anſwer, ου
μα δι, αλλ ασθενει; "He is not dead, but he is
ſick."

Theſe few quotations will give the Reader
ſome faint idea of the originality and ſpirit,
of the ſublimity and energy, of the eloquence of DEMOSTHENES.   We ſhall next
produce

produce a few paffages from the Orations of CICERO, which will alfo ferve to illuftrate the preceding remarks on original Rhetorical Genius.

The *Roman* Orator having, with the other fenators, obtained certain information of the execrable confpiracy of CATILINE, breaks forth in a torrent of abrupt, vehement, and rapid eloquence, in the following addrefs to this chief of the confpirators, whom he pointed out to the whole affembled fenate *.

So

---

* " Quoufque tandem abutere Catilina patientia
" noftra? Quamdiu etiam furor ifte tuus nos eludet?
" Quem ad finem fefe effrænata ja#abit audacia?
" Nihilne te no#urnum præfidium palatii, nihil urbis
" vigiliæ, nihil timor populi, nihil concurfus bonorum
" omnium, nihil hic munitiffimus habendi fenatus lo-
" cus, nihil horum ora vultufque moverunt? Patere
" tua confilia non fentis? conftri#am jam horum om-
" nium confcientia teneri conjurationem tuam non vi-
" des? Quid proxima, quid fuperiore no#e egeris,
" ubi fueris, quos convocaveris, quid confilii ceperis
" quem

So energetic, so particular, and so pointed an accusation, could not fail to confound even

---

" quem nostrum ignorare arbitraris? O tempora! O
" mores! Senatus hæc intelligit, Consul videt, hic
" tamen vivit! Vivit? Imo etiam in senatum venit;
" sit publici consilii particeps; notat & designat oculis
" ad cædem unumquemque nostrum †.

" How long, CATILINE, will you abuse our pa-
tience? How long shall your desperate fury elude our
vengeance? For what end does your unbridled auda-
ciousness thus triumph? Has not the nocturnal garison
of mount *Palatine,* have not the watches of the city,
has not the fear of the people, has not the united con-
coarse of all good men, has not this guarded senate-
house, have not the venerable countenances of those
conscript Fathers, have not all these the power to dis-
arm thy rage, and to soften thy unrelenting heart?
Do you imagine your designs are not discovered? Do
not you see that your conspiracy is baffled by the time-
ly knowledge of all these Senators? What you did
the last, what the preceding night, where you was,
whom you called together, what resolutions you formed, is there any one here, think you, ignorant of?
O times! O manners! The Senate is made acquainted with these things, the Consul sees them;
yet this wretch lives. Lives! did I say? Nay, he hath

† Orat. prim. in *Cat.*

had

even the audacious CATILINE. CICERO,
we may obferve in the above inftance, de-
parts from a general rule, which, with
great propriety, requires for the moft part,
that the exordium of an oration be cool
and difpaffionate. The obfervance of this
rule indeed depends upon the fubject and
the occafion; and furely the occafion of the
oration to which we refer, demanded the
utmoft vehemence and energy.

The Orator tranfgreffes the fame rule
with equal propriety in his fourth Oration
againft CATILINE, which is animated and
interefting from the beginning. Having,
in the introduction to his difcourfe, acknowledged in a very graceful manner the grate-
ful fenfe he had of the Senate's concern for
his fafety, he comes, by a natural tranfi-

---

had the daring infolence to enter the fenate-houfe, and
to fhare in the public deliberations, while he fingles
out every one of us with his eyes, and deftines us to
flaughter."

tion,

tion, to touch upon his own dangerous fituation, the defcription of which is wrought up with the higheft art, as it recals at once to the remembrance of his hearers, the various labours and hazards he had undergone for the fake of his country, in the part he had acted in the detection of CATILINE's confpiracy *.

---

* " Ego fum ille Conful, Patres confcripti, cui non
" forum in quo omnis æquitas continetur : non cam-
" pus, confularibus aufpiciis confecratus : non curia,
" fummum auxilium omnium gentium : non domus,
" commune perfugium : non lectus, ad quietem da-
" tus : non denique hæc fedes honoris, fella curu-
" lis, unquam vacua mortis periculo atque infidiis
" fuit."

" I, confcript Fathers, am that Conful, to whom not the forum in which juftice is diftributed ; not the martial field confecrated by confular aufpices ; not the Senate, the chief aid of all nations ; not the houfe, every one's common refuge ; not the bed, defigned for repofe ; not, finally, this feat of honour, this curule chair, have ever afforded fecurity from the dangers and the fnares of death."

The

The Orator then proceeds to enumerate the services he had done to the commonwealth in the investigation of the above-mentioned conspiracy, as well as to point out the risk with which they were performed; a relation, that great as those services were, would, it must be confessed, have come better from another mouth. One is indeed sorry to find the vanity of CICERO, which was his distinguishing foible, displayed in so glaring a manner in this, as well as in several other instances; but let candour draw the veil over his foibles, in consideration of his eloquence and merit.

It would be a material omission, while we are producing specimens of CICERO's oratorical talents, to overlook his celebrated oration for his friend MILO, accused as the author of the death of CLODIUS; an oration in which TULLY hath exhibited an astonishing display both of his reasoning and pathetic talents, and in which he hath united Imagination,

Imagination, Judgment and Art, in the higheft degree. After having proved by an accurate and diftinct detail of circum- ftances, urged with great force of argument, that MILO could have no defign upon the life of CLODIUS, but that, on the contrary, the latter had confpired againft the life of MILO, in the attempt to execute which in- tention he was himfelf flain; the Orator breaks out into a fublime apoftrophe, ad- dreffed to the altars and groves which CLO- DIUS had polluted by his impurities, im- puting the original caufe of his death to their juft vengeance, and that of the Gods whofe rites he had violated †.

It

---

† " Vos enim jam Albani luci atque tumuli, vos
" inquam imploro atque teftor, vofque Albanorum
" obrutæ aræ, facrorum populi Romani fociæ & æqua-
" les, quas ille præceps amentia, cæfis, proftratisque
" fanctiffimis lucis, fubftructionum infanis molibus
" oppreflerat: veftræ tum aræ, veftræ religiones vi-
" guerunt, veftra vis valuit, quam ille omni fcelere
" polluerat: tuque ex tuo edito monte, Latialis fancte
" Jupiter, cujus ille lacus, nemora, finesque fæpe omni
" nefario

It is the privilege of Eloquence, as well as Poetry, to employ thofe figures which give

---

" nefario ftupro & fcelere macularat, aliquando ad
" eum puniendum oculos aperuiftis : vobis illæ, vobis
" veftro in confpectu feræ, fed juftæ tamen, & debitæ
" pœnæ folutæ funt."

" Ye hills and groves of *Alba*, and you *Alban* altars, memorials of the *Roman* rites, and coeval with the *Roman* name, facred groves and altars, rafed by his defperate madnefs, and on the ruins of which he reared thofe impious piles ; you I implore, and call to witnefs his guilt.  Your rites polluted by his crimes, your worfhip profaned, your authority infulted, have at laft difplayed their vengeance ; and thou, divine *Latian* Jove, whofe lakes, woods and boundaries, he had fo often defiled with his deteftable impurities, didft at laft open thy eyes, and look down from thy high and holy hill to punifh this profligate wretch ; to you his blood was due, and in your fight the long delayed vengeance was at laft inflicted !"

The learned Reader will obferve, that the Author hath taken confiderable liberty in the tranflation of the above paffage.  As the principal thing to be regarded in every verfion is to tranflate the fenfe, and, if poffible, transfufe the fpirit of an Author from one language into another, which, confidering the different idioms of languages, is impoffible to execute, by rendering

give life, motion, and fenfe to inanimate
matter. Such figures, when judicioufly
introduced and properly fupported, give
inexpreffible dignity, vivacity, and energy
to rhetorical compofition; as they always
indicate not only Originality, but likewife
great Sublimity and Strength of GENIUS.
Every Reader muft perceive the difference
betwixt faying that CLODIUS was flain by
the juft vengeance of the Gods for his
profanation of· their groves and altars, and
a folemn addrefs to thofe hills, groves,
and altars, as well as the Deities who
prefided over them, by a ftriking profopopœia, as if they were real perfons, calling them to witnefs his guilt, and imput-
ing his death to their refentment upon

dering word for word; he found himfelf obliged, in
order to do fome kind of juftice to the original, to
admit fome tranfpofitions and circumlocutions, which,
though they have occafioned an alteration in the order and arrangement of the periods, have however
enabled him, as he conceives, lefs imperfe&ly to exhibit the fenfe.

account

account of their violated rites. In the firſt caſe we are unmoved, in the laſt we are tranſported with aſtoniſhment at the novelty, vivacity, and grandeur of the repreſentation.

We ſhall ſubjoin two ſhort paſſages, taken from the end of this Oration, as ſpecimens of CICERO's talents in moving the paſſions of his hearers, a qualification the moſt eſſential of all others in an Orator. One may perceive him gradually warming towards the concluſion of his diſcourſe, till he works himſelf up to the higheſt fervour and energy of paſſion. We can ſcarce conceive an addreſs more animated and perſuaſive, or more happily adapted to rouſe the affections of the Soldiers, who guarded the Aſſembly, than the following *.

The

* " Vos, vos appello, fortiſſimî viri, qui multum " pro republica ſanguinem effudiſtis : vos in viri & in

" civis

The Orator concludes his difcourfe with
a panegyric on the virtues of MILO, reprefenting

---

" civis invicti appello periculo, centuriones, vosque
" milites : vobis non modo infpectantibus, fed etiam
" armatis & huic judicio præfidentibus, hæc tanta
" virtus ex hac urbe expelletur ? exterminabitur ? pro-
" jicietur ? O me miferum ! O infelicem ! revocare
" tu me in patriam, Milo, potuifti per hos : ego te in
" patria per eofdem retinere non potero ? Quid re-
" fpondebo liberis meis, qui te parentem alterum pu-
" tant ? Quid tibi, Q. Frater, qui nunc abes, conforti
" mecum temporum illorum ? me non potuiffe Milo-
" nis falutem tueri per eofdem, per quos noftram ille
" fervaffet ? "

" You, you bravest of men, I call, who have
fo much of your blood for the commonwealth. You
centurions, and you foldiers I invoke, while the fate
of an unconquered man and citizen is in fufpenfe.
Shall fo much virtue be banifhed, exterminated, caft
out from this city, while you are not only fpectators
of this trial, but the armed guardians of it ? Unhappy
and miferable that I am ! Could you, MILO, recal me
from banifhment into my native country by means of
thefe men ? and fhall not I be able to preferve you in
your country by their means ? What fhall I fay to my
children, who regard you as another parent ? what to
thee, my abfent brother QUINTUS, who didft participate

fenting at the fame time, in a very animated manner, both the lofs and difgrace which would redound to his country from his banifhment †.

Thefe

---

pate with me in the dangers of thofe unhappy times? that I could not infure the fafety of Milo by the fame perfons by whom he fecured ours?"

† " Hiccine vir patriæ natus, ufquam nifi in patria
" morietur? aut, fi forte, pro patria? Hujus vos ani-
" mi monumenta retinebitis: corporis in Italia nullum
" fepulchrum effe patiemeni? hunc fua quifquam fen-
" tentia ex hac urbe expellet, quem omnes urbes ex-
" pulfum, a vobis ad fe vocabunt? O terram illam
" beatam, quæ hunc virum exceperit! hanc ingratam,
" fi ejecerit; miferam, fi amiferit! Sed finis fit. Ne-
" que enim præ lacrymis jam loqui poffum: & hic fe
" lacrymis defendi vetat."

" Shall this man, born for his country, die any where but in his country? or, if the Gods order it fo, for his country? Will you retain the monuments of his genius, and allow no fepulchre to his body in *Italy*? Shall any one by his vote banifh a man from this city, whom, once banifhed, all other cities will invite to refide in them? O happy land, which fhall receive this excellent perfon; ungrateful that fhall ba-

Q 2                         nifh

These quotations from the Orations of
DEMOSTHENES and CICERO, though they
cannot give us a proper idea of the aftonifhing eloquence of thofe celebrated Orators,
which it is impoffible to exhibit by a few
unconnected extracts, will however ferve to
fhew the power of original Genius in Eloquence, the chief purpofe for which they
were produced; and that this rare talent,
wherever it is found, will always difcover
itfelf, as we have already feen, in employing the moft fublime, the moft fplendid,
and the moft ftriking figures in compofition,
as well as in inventing the moft furprifing,
and at the fame time the moft proper topics
of perfuafion on every fubject, which it will
difplay in all their force, and urge with irrefiftible efficacy.

---

nifh him! miferable that fhall lofe him! But I conclude. Nor will my tears allow me to proceed; and
the perfon in whofe caufe I fpeak, confcious as he is
of his own innocence, difdains the aid and importu-
nity of tears."

It

It is impoffible to avoid obferving on this fubject, that there is no art in which the Moderns come fo far fhort of the Ancients as in that of Eloquence. We muft not however omit to take fome notice of modern Eloquence; and here it would be inexcufable intirely to pafs over the *French* Orators, who, though it cannot he pretended that they have equaled the illuftrious Ancients above-mentioned, have however difcovered a high degree of rhetorical Genius. We fhall lay before the Reader a few extracts from the Sermons of BOURDALOUE and MASSILLON, paffing over at prefent BOSSUET and SAURIN, whom we fhall have occafion to take fome notice of in another part of this Effay.

BOURDALOUE, defcribing the future punifhment of the wicked, of which he reprefents their banifhment from the immediate prefence of the Deity as an effential part, inquires what is implied in the idea of fuch a feparation. The Reader will obferve that

Q 3                              his

his reasoning upon this point is spirited and
emphatical : " Car qu' est ce qu' d' etre
" separe de Dieu ? Ah ! Chretiens, quelle
" parole ! la comprenez vous ? Separe de
" Dieu, c'est a dire, prive absolument de
" Dieu. Separé de Dieu, c'est a dire, con-
" damné à n' avoir plus de Dieu, si ce n'est
" un Dieu ennemi, un Dieu vengeur. Se-
" paré de Dieu, c'est a dire, dechu de tout
" droit à l'eternelle posséffion du premier de
" tous les etres, du Souverain etre qui est
" Dieu *." After having insisted on the
certainty of the future punishment of the
wicked, the Preacher, astonished at the indifference of mankind to this great truth,
exclaims ; " Est ce stupidité ? est ce inad-
" vertence ? est ce fureur ? est ce enchante-
" ment ? Crayons-nous ce point fondamen-
" tal du Christianisme ; ne le croyons-nous
" pas ? si nous le croyons ? Ou est notre
" sageffe ? si nous ne le croyons pas, ou est

---

* Vol. V. Serm. 2.

" notre

" notre religion? Je dis plus: fi nous ne
" le croyons pas? que croyons-nous donc?
" puisqu'il n'eft rien de plus croyable, rien
" de plus formellement revelé par la parole
" divine, rien de plus folidement fondé dans
" la raifon humaine, rien dont la creance
" foit plus neceffaire pour le tenir les hom-
" mes dans le devoir, rien fur quoi le doute
" leur foit plus pernicieux, puisqu'il les
" porte a tous les defordres †."

MASSILLON, whom we may juftly regard as the Prince of modern Orators, difplays great power over the paffions in many
of his Sermons; particularly in that " on
the Death of a Sinner," where he rifes to
an uncommon pitch of Eloquence. His
defcription of this unhappy man in the laft
agony of nature, is equally picturefque and
affecting: " Alors le pecheur mourant ne
" trouvant plus dans le fouvenir du pafsé

---

† Vol. V. Serm. 2.

" que

" que des regrets que l'accablent ; dans tout
" que ce passé a ses yeux, que des images
" qui l'affligent ; dans la pensée de l'avenir
" que des horreurs qui l'epouvantent : ne
" sachant plus a qui avoir recours ; ni
" aux creatures, qui lui echappent ; ni au
" monde, qui s'evanouit ; ni aux hommes,
" qui ne sauroient le delivrer de la mort ;
" ni au Dieu juste, qu'il regarde comme
" un ennemi declaré, dont il ne doit plus
" attendre d'indulgence ; il se roule dans
" ses propres horreurs ; il se tourmente, il
" s'agite pour faire la mort qui le saisit, ou
" du moins pour se fuir lui-meme : il sort
" de ses yeux mourans, je ne sai quoi de
" sombre & de farouche, qui exprime les
" fureurs de son ame : il pousse du fond
" de sa tristesse des paroles entrecoupées de
" sanglots, qu'on n'entend qu'a demi ; &
" qu'on ne sai si c'est le desespoir ou le re-
" pentir qui les a formée ; il jette sur un
" Dieu crucifié des regards affreux, & qui
" laissent douter si c'est la crainte, ou l'espe-
" rance, la haine ou l'amour qu'ils expri-
" ment ;

"ment; il entre dans des saisissemens ou
" l'on ignore si c'est le corps qui se dissoud
" ou l'ame qui sent l'approche de son Juge :
" il soupire profondement & l'on ne sait si
" c'est le souvenir de ses crimes, qui lui ar-
" rache ses sonpirs ou le desespoir de quitter
" la vie. Enfin, au milieu de ses tristes
" efforts, ses yeux se fixent, ses traites
" changent, son visage se defigure ; sa
" bouche livide s'entre ouvre d'elle meme :
" tout son esprit fremit ; & par ce dernier
" effort son ame infortunie s'arrache comme
" a regret de ce corps de bouc, tombe entre
" les mains de Dieu, & se trouve seule aux
" pieds du tribunal redoutable ‡." In the
same Sermon, taking a view of the death
of a good man, by way of contrast, we
meet with the following eloquent exclama-
tion : " Grand Dieu ! que de lumiere !
" que de paix ! que de transports heureux !
" que de saints mouvements d'amour ! de

---

‡ Vol. I. Serm. 2.

" joie,

" joie, de confiance, d'actions de grace,
" se passent alors dans cette ame fidele ! sa
" foi si renouvelle ; son amour & s'enflam-
" me ; sa ferveur s'excite ; sa componction
" se reveille."

It is very astonishing, that while our own country can claim the honour of having given birth to several eminent Poets, and many great Philosophers, it should not have given birth to one accomplished Orator ; and that, while it can boast of having produced an equal to HOMER in the person of MILTON, it should never once have produced, either in the eloquence of the Pulpit or the Bar, a rival to DEMOST-HENES or CICERO ! Indeed, when we consider the great variety of qualifications, both natural and acquired, necessary to constitute a complete Orator, we cannot expect they should often be united in one person ; though that this union should never have happened in any one instance in modern times, must be confessed to be really wonderful. What is still more surprising, is, that in the vast multitude of Sermons, which this age and the last hath produced, many of which abound with solid reasoning, as some are distinguished by the elegance of their stile, we have seen very few attempts at genuine Eloquence. The Author however takes a particular pleasure in observing, that in some Sermons lately published, there are to be found several distinguished specimens of true oratorial Genius; and he makes no doubt that he shall oblige most of his Readers, by giving a few short extracts from them.

In a Sermon delivered before his Majesty's Commissioner to the Church of *Scotland*, in *May* 1760, by Dr FORDYCE, and published at *Edinburgh*, the Preacher, after having shewn in a very eloquent manner the folly and infamy of unlawful pleasure, proceeds to take a view of the misery attending it; in doing which he paints the voluptuary in a very alarming situation, in the immediate

diate profpect of his diffolution. Let the candid Reader judge whether the following paffage does not exhibit a very ftriking picture of the ftate of an abandoned Libertine in that awful crifis : " O the fhudderings, " the ftrong reluctance, the unimaginable " convulfions that feize his nature, as he " ftands lingering on the tremendous preci- " pice! He wifhes for annihilation, which " he often tried to believe in, but could " never ferioufly be convinced of. The " dreadful alternative intirely mifgives him. " He meditates the devouring abyfs of eter- " nity : he recoils as he eyes it." There is a particular propriety in the fhort fentences which conclude this paffage; and they are as ftrongly expreffive of the fituation they are intended to defcribe, as any I ever remember to have read. After finifhing the defcription in a few more fentences, the Author very naturally and very emphatically afks, " Is this the man that laughed the " children of wifdom and temperance to " fcorn? Is he of the fame opinion, think " ye

" ye, at the laſt?" Then follows a reflection, as pathetic in itſelf as the language is
beautiful in which it is expreſſed: " Ah, how
" different his ſentiments and language in
" the bower of pleaſure, and on the bed of
" death!" The Reader will find ſeveral
other ſtrokes of true Eloquence in this Sermon, as well as in the other occaſional Diſ-
courſes publiſhed by the ſame Author.

There is a paſſage much to our purpoſe in
a ſmall collection of Sermons, lately publiſhed
by Dr OGILVIE; who, though he has dedicated his Genius principally to Poetry, in
which he has acquired a high and juſt reputation, poſſeſſes at the ſame time, in an uncommon degree, the eſſential qualifications
of the Orator. In one of the Sermons
above referred to, we meet with the following bold and ſublime apoſtrophe: " O ye
" immortal ſpirits! who are at this moment
" exulting in the regions of felicity, with
" what ſuperior indifference do you look
" down on the little cares, the abſurd pre-
" ſumption,

" fumption, the inconfiftent characters of
" mankind! You who can trace the fecret,
" the imperceptible fteps, by which Provi-
" dence hath conducted you to your eternal
" inheritance, muft fometimes look with
" an eye of pity on your furviving friends,
" dancing the fame tirefome round of giddy
" pleafure, and prepofteroufly afcribing to
" themfelves thofe actions, to which you fee
" them gradually conducted by a fuperior
" hand!" This abrupt and fublime addrefs
is a noble effort of elevated Genius.

The *Englifh* Preachers are, it is certain,
more diftinguifhed by their JUSTNESS of
SENTIMENT, and STRENGTH of REASONING,
than by their ORATORIAL POWERS, or talents of AFFECTING the PASSIONS. More
folicitous to CONVINCE than PERSUADE, they
choofe to employ their abilities in endeavouring to imprefs the mind with a fenfe of
the truths they deliver by the force of argumentation, inftead of roufing the affections
by the energy of their Eloquence.    But
                                    though

though we meet with no examples in their writings of thofe ftrokes of paffion which PENETRATE and CLEAVE the heart at once, or of that rapid overpowering Eloquence, which carries every thing before it like a torrent; yet there may be found in their Sermons many inftances of the moft fhining and delicate beauties of Rhetoric, fuch as indicate great FERTILITY, though not equal FORCE of Imagination. Upon account of thefe beauties, SEED and ATTERBURY claim a particular preeminence. A DIGNITY of SENTIMENT, a SMOOTHNESS, and EASY ELEGANCE of DICTION, are remarkably confpicuous in the Works of both; and the Sermons of the former are adorned with the richeft variety of beautiful and well-adapted imagery, that I have ever met with in a profe writer. He excels peculiarly in the application of the metaphor. Let the following paffage ftand as an example of his dexterity in varying and appropriating this pleafing figure. Speaking of the advantages of a life uniformly good, he adds, " How
" would

" would this SETTLE the FERMENT of our
" youthful paffions, and SWEETEN the laft
" DREGS of our advanced age! how would
" this make our lives yield the CALMEST fa-
" tisfaction, as fome flowers fhed the moft
" FRAGRANT ODOURS juft at the clofe of the
" day! And perhaps there is no better way
" to prevent a DEADNESS and FLATNESS of
" fpirit from fucceeding, when the BRISKNESS
" of our paffions goes off, than to acquire
" an early tafte for thofe fpiritual delights,
" whofe LEAF withers not, and whofe ver-
" dure remains in the winter of our days †."
Having fhewn the infufficiency of the mere
light of nature to clear up our doubts, or re-
move our fears, arifing from the apprehenfion of future punifhment for thofe crimes
of which we are confcious, he concludes
with an obfervation, in which, by perfonify-
ing Reafon, he rifes to a confiderable degree
of Eloquence: " Here then Reafon was at
" the end of its line; it ftood upon the fhore,

" eyed

" eyed the vaft ocean of Eternity which lay
" before it, faw a little, imagined a great
" deal; but clouds and darknefs foon ter-
" minated its narrow profpect *." To thefe
we fhall only add one other paffage from
the Sermon in which we found the preceding, as it will fhew what additional grace
the moft noble fentiments may derive from
a feries of imagery equally appofite and beautiful.    " Carry thy eye upwards to that
" bleffed place, where thy nature fhall be as
" it were caft anew, purified from all droffy
" mixtures and coarfe alloys of human
" frailty, but brightened and refined as to
" the fterling luftre and genuine excellen-
" cies of the foul.   Here is one continued
" repetition of the fame unfatisfactory ob-
" jects, and there is nothing new under the
" fun; but there, far perhaps above the
" fun, new fcenes, new beings, new won-
" ders, new joys will prefent themfelves to

---

* Vol. I. page 321.

R                    " our

" our enlarged view. Look then upon this
" world as one wide ocean, where many are
" fhipwrecked and irrecoverably loft, more
" are toffed and fluctuating; but none can
" fecure to themfelves for any confiderable
" time a future undifturbed calm: the fhip
" however is ftill under fail, and whether
" the weather be fair or foul, we are every
" minute making nearer approaches to, and
" muft fhortly reach the fhore; and may it
" be the haven where we would be ✝!"

The Bifhop of *Rochefter*, defcribing the
happinefs of an acquaintance with God,
fums up the whole with the following beautiful and foothing reflection; which is well
calculated to infpire that ferenity of mind,
which flows from the acquaintance he recommends. " O! the fweet contentment,
" the tranquillity, and profound reft of
" mind that he enjoys, who is a friend of
" God, and to whom God therefore is a

---

✝ Vol. I. page 345.

" friend;

" friend; who hath gotten loofe from all
" meaner purfuits, and is regardlefs of all
" lower advantages that interfere with his
" defire of knowing and loving God, and of
" being known and beloved by him; who
" lives as in his fight always, looks up to
" him in every ftep of his conduct, imitates
" him to the beft of his power, believes him
" without doubt, and obeys him without re-
" ferve *," &c.   In his Sermon on the anni-
verfary of the Martyrdom of King CHARLES
the Firft, he conveys to us a lively idea of
the fufferings of that unhappy Prince, by a
fublime metaphor: " The paffage through
" this *Red-fea* was bloody, but fhort; a di-
" vine Hand ftrengthened him in it, and
" conducted him through it; and he foon
" reached the fhore of blifs and immorta-
" lity †."

---

* ATTERBURY's Sermons, vol. II. p. 198.
† *Ibid.* vol. IV. p. 13.

To the examples above produced, I take the liberty to subjoin one other paffage of a different kind; but which, by every real judge, will be acknowledged to deferve a diftinguifhed regard, fince it is animated with all the boldnefs and enthufiafm of the Orator and the Patriot. The paffage I have in my eye, is faid to have been part of a fpeech delivered in the *Britifh* Senate, by a late great Commoner, upon a very popular occafion; and that it is conceived in an high ftile of Eloquence, I will venture to affirm. " I never " feared any man, nor paid court to any fet " of men. I have worfhipped the Goddefs " Liberty alone, ever fince I drew my breath. " I hope to do fo in a land of liberty while " that breath remains. And when the fpirit " fhall have forfaken this crazy tabernacle, " I pray my Guardian Angel to throw my " afhes on that fpot of the globe where Free- " dom reigns." What the effect of this part of the fpeech was in the *Britifh* Senate, I have not heard; but I am well perfuaded that it would have been applauded in the *Roman* Forum,

Forum, or by an *Athenian* Affembly; and though perhaps it is of too elevated a kind to fuit the cold and correct Genius of a modern Critic, it would have afforded a fubject of Panegyric to Longinus or Quintilian.

It is not our prefent bufinefs to inquire into the caufes of our deficiency in Oratory, as we intend, in a following fection, to hazard fome reflections on the fubject. In the mean time we may obferve in general, that moft of our modern pretenders to Eloquence feem to have confidered mankind in the fame light in which Voltaire regarded the celebrated Dr Clarke, as mere reafoning machines: they feem to have confidered them as purely intellectual, void of paffion and fenfibility. This ftrange miftake may perhaps be fuppofed to be partly the effect of the philofophical fpirit of the times, which, like all other prevailing modes, is fubject to its deliriums; certain however it is, that while man remains a compound being, confifting

R 3

fifting of reafon and paffion, his actions will always be prompted by the latter, in whatever degree his opinions may be influenced by the former. So long however as men continue ignorant of the nature, and indifferent to the ftudy of Eloquence, there is little reafon to hope for the difplay of Originality of GENIUS in this noble art. Neverthelefs if we confider its nature, its extent, and the improvements of which it is fufceptible, we fhall have abundant reafon to conclude, that this talent may ftill be difplayed to the utmoft advantage, as doubtlefs it will be in every age, when circumftances concur to favour its exertion. There are innumerable avenues to the human heart, innumerable methods of captivating the affections, of roufing the paffions, and influencing the will; and powerful as was the eloquence of DEMOSTHENES and CICERO, thofe great Orators, with all their admirable invention, have not exhaufted all the treafures of their art. It will indeed be extremely difficult to invent means of raifing and allaying, of foothing

and

and irritating, of agitating and inflaming
the paffions of mankind, different from what
have been practifed by thofe immortal Orators above-mentioned; and perhaps it will
be ftill more difficult to improve the means
which they have invented and fo fuccefsfully
ufed. To accomplifh thefe purpofes however is certainly not impoffible *, and therefore ought not to be defpaired of.

Let us in the next place obferve the efforts
of ORIGINAL GENIUS in Mufic †.

The

---

* " Sed cur deficiat animus ? Natura enim perfectum
" Oratorem effe non prohibet : turpiterque defperatur
" quicquid fieri poteft." QUINTIL. *Inftit.* lib. i.
cap. 10.

† Mufic appears to have been in great efteem among
the ancients. QUINTILIAN in particular beftows the
higheft encomiums on this divine art; and tells us,
that it was cultivated by the greateft and wifeft men of
antiquity:

" Nam

The talents of a PERFORMER, and a MAS-
TER and COMPOSER of Mufic, are very different. To conftitute the firft, a nice mufical ear, and a dexterity of performance
acquired by habit, are the fole requifites.
To conftitute the laft, not only a nice mufical ear, but an exquifite fenfibility of paffion, together with a peculiar CONFORMA-

---

" Nam quis ignorat Muficen (ut de hac primum
" loquar) tantum jam illis antiquis temporibus non
" ftudii modo, verum etiam venerationis habuiffe, ut
" iidem & Mufici & vates, & fapientes judicarentur?
" Mittam alios: Orpheus & Linus; quorum utrum-
" que Diis genitum, alterum vero quod rudes quoque
" atque agreftes animos admiratione mulceret, non
" feras modo, fed faxa.etiam fylvasque duxiffe, pofte-
" ritatis memoriæ traditum eft. Et teftes Timagenes
" auctor eft, omnium in literis ftudiorum antiquiffi-
" mam Muficen extitiffe; & teftimonio funt clariffimi
" Poetæ, apud quos inter regalia convivia laudes He-
" roum ac Deorum ad citharas canebantur." *Inftit.*
lib. i. cap. 10.

The fame Author juftly obferves, in another part of
his excellent Work, that the pleafure which we derive
from Mufic is founded in nature: " Natura ducimur
" ad modos." *Lib. ix. cap. 4.*

TION

TION of Genius to this particular art, are indifpenfibly neceffary. Though all the liberal Arts are indebted to Imagination in common, a talent for each of them refpectively depends upon the peculiar MODIFICATION and ADAPTATION of this faculty to the feveral RESPECTIVE Arts. Thus the Poet, having by the force of Imagination formed lively images of the objects he propofes to defcribe, thinks only of expreffing his ideas in fmooth and harmonious numbers; the Painter, having the fame vivid conception of every object, is wholly intent on exhibiting a reprefentation of them in colours, as if he had no other method of conveying his ideas; and the Mufician, having his head filled with crotchets and concords, airs and fonatas, employs his Imagination intirely in combining a variety of founds, and trying their power, in order to conftitute harmony. A mufical Genius naturally exerts itfelf in exercifes of this kind, and is indicated by them. In this art likewife it muft be confeffed, that confiderable fcope is afforded for the exertions

tions

tions even of ORIGINAL GENIUS. Every masterly Composer of Music must feel, in the most intense and exquisite degree, the various emotions, which, by his compositions, he attempts to excite in the minds of others. Even before he begins to compose a piece of music, he must work himself up to that transport of passion, which he desires to express and to communicate in his piece. In effectuating this purpose, Imagination operates very powerfully, by awakening in his own mind those particular affections, that are correspondent to the airs he is meditating; and by raising each of these to that tone of sensibility, and that fervor of passion, which is most favourable to composition. This fervor and enthusiasm of passion, may be termed the inspiration of Music; and is the principal quality which gives it such an irresistible empire over the human heart. The maxim of HORACE,

*Si vis me flere, dolendum est primum ipsi tibi.*
Would you have me participate your pain ?
First teach yourself to feel the woes you feign;

is

is a rule as neceſſary to be obſerved by a
Compoſer of Muſic, in thoſe ſtrains which
are intended to excite ſympathy and grief,
as by a Tragic Poet, who would excite the
ſame emotions.

We may farther obſerve, that as an arbitrary combination of ſounds can never produce the harmony, much leſs the expreſſion
of Muſic, any more than a random aſſem-
blage of words can make an elegant and
connected poem or oration; ſo Imagination,
under the direction of a tuneful ear, muſt
aſſiſt the muſical Artiſt in adopting and
combining thoſe ſounds only, which may affect the paſſions in the manner he intends.

It muſt be granted indeed, that the efforts of Imagination diſcovered in Muſic,
though not inconſiderable, are by no means
ſo extraordinary as in any of the Arts above-
mentioned. The exerciſe of this quality
ſeems in Muſic to be ſomewhat confined,
being neceſſarily ſubjected to, and under the
direction

direction of the ear, by which it is affifted;
whereas in Poetry and Eloquence, it is abfolute and unbounded, as every idea of the
mind may be defcribed; and in Painting, it
is very little reftrained, fince moft of them
may be delineated.

After all, when we confider how many
ways there are of affecting the human heart
by the power of founds; how the affections
may be melted into tendernefs, or kindled
into tranfport; how the paffions may be
raifed and allayed, agitated and inflamed;
how they may be elevated to the higheft
pitch of fublimity, fired with heroic ardor,
or lulled in the voluptuous languor of effe-
minate luxury; we may be fufficiently convinced, that there remains an extenfive field
yet unoccupied for the difplay of ORIGINA-
LITY of GENIUS, in the noble art of which
we are treating. It is much to be regretted,
that our modern Mafters in this art have in
general endeavoured to render their compofitions pleafing to the ear, rather than affecting

fecting to the heart; that they have ftudied the foft and delicate graces, rather than the fublime and animated expreffion of Mufic; and that by attempting to heighten its melody, they have in a great meafure deprived it of the energy and eloquence of paffion, and thereby rendered mufical concerts rather a delicious gratification, than an ufeful and exalted entertainment.

We fhall confider laftly, how far ORIGINALITY of GENIUS may be difcovered in Architecture.

It muft be confeffed, that no improvements have been made in this art by our modern Architects, whofe greateft ambition and excellence it hath been, to underftand and to copy thofe venerable remains of ancient Architecture; which have efcaped the rage of Barbarians, or withftood the ravages of time. Thofe auguft monuments of antiquity, which have been the wonder and admiration of ages, have been confidered, ed, by the moſt ingenious artiſts themſelves, as complete Models of Architecture, from which nothing can be taken, and to which nothing can be added; and are in fact ſuch as few of them have ever equaled, and none of them (whether through want of ability, or want of ambition) have ever excelled. Great veneration is unqueſtionably due to ancient Genius. The Ancients have indeed been our Maſters in the liberal Arts; and their productions deſerve our higheſt commendations: yet let us not ſhew them a blind and ſuperſtitious reverence. Abſolute perfection is incompatible with the works of man; and while we regard the works of the Ancients as ſo perfect, that we deſpair of excelling them, the conſequence will be, that we ſhall never be able to equal them: the ORIGINAL will always be preferable to the COPY. We have already animadverted on this too ſervile deference to antiquity *; and ſhall only here remark,

---

* Book I. Section II.

that

that this difpofition is highly unfavourable to the improvement of any of the Arts; and that a diffident timidity will always prove a greater difcouragement, as well as obftruction to Originality of Genius, than prefumptuous temerity. The one, in afpiring beyond its fphere, may indeed tumble from its towering height; but the other, cautious and fearful, will fcarce ever rife from the ground.

Where few attempts therefore are made to excel, original Genius cannot be much difplayed. It is neverthelefs certain, that great fcope is afforded for the difplay of it in the Art we are fpeaking of, in which an unreftrained exercife is allowed to the faculty of Imagination, becaufe the forms of elegance and gracefulnefs, of beauty and grandeur, which it is its province to invent, are innumerable. Where this faculty is reftrained, and the ambition and exertion of Artifts are confined to the imitation of certain Models invented by others, there it cannot

not operate in any confiderable degree; for IMITATION will ever be found a bar to ORIGINALITY. A pretty extenfive Imagination, we confefs, may be exerted in affembling together the detached parts of one great defign; and when thefe are united together in the conftruction of an edifice of confummate fymmetry and beauty, we allow the building to be an illuftrious monument of the Genius and Tafte of the Artift who defigned it: but where the whole is only ingenioufly collected, and no part invented, a claim to ORIGINALITY of Genius can by no means be admitted in his favour.

A Genius for Architecture truly ORIGINAL, will, by the native force and plaftic power of Imagination, ftrike out for itfelf new and furprifing Models in this Art; and, by its combining faculty, will felect out of the infinite variety of ideal forms that float in the mind, thofe of the Grand and Beautiful, which it will unite in one confummate as well as uncommon defign. We
have

have already obferved, that every original
Genius, whether in Architecture or in any
other of the liberal Arts, is peculiarly diftinguifhed by a powerful bias to INVENTION.
It was this bias which we may call the in-
ftinctive, infuppreffible Impulfe of Genius,
whofe fpontaneous efforts defigned thofe ftupendous Gothic ftructures, that appear fo
magnificent in their ruins.   The Architects,
who firft planned thofe edifices, though
unacquainted with the polite Arts, or with
the *Grecian* and *Roman* Architecture, were
doubtlefs great Originals in their profeffion,
fince they planned them by the unaided
ftrength of their own Genius.   Their un-
tutored imaginations prompted them to af-
pire to the Solemn, the Vaft, and the Wonderful; and allowing an unbounded fcope to
the exercife of this faculty, they were enabled to give to their buildings that awful,
though irregular grandeur, which elevates
the mind, and produces the moft pleafing
aftonifhment.   Thefe Gothic edifices fhew
the inventive power of the human mind in
S                    a ftriking

a striking light, and are sufficient to convince us, that excellence in Architecture was
not confined to the *Greeks* and *Romans*, but
may be sometimes displayed among a people
in other respects barbarous.

Though it is impossible to point out the
particular tracks which an ORIGINAL GE-
NIUS in Architecture will pursue, in endeavouring to improve the art he professes, as
those tracks are so various, and the natural
powers of Artists are so different; yet we
may remark, that after all the improvements which Architecture received in the
age of PERICLES and of AUGUSTUS, it seems
susceptible of one important improvement,
from the union of the awful Gothic grandeur with the majestic simplicity and graceful elegance of the *Grecian* and *Roman* edifices; and that by such an union ORIGINA-
LITY of GENIUS in this art might be signally
displayed.

We

We shall conclude this section with observing, that though the simplest and earliest periods of society are favourable to original descriptive Poetry, which we shall immediately endeavour to shew, and Eloquence will always be exerted in its utmost power under a Democratical form of government, during the reign of Liberty and public Spirit; Painting and Architecture will in general attain their highest degree of improvement, in the most advanced state of society, under the irradiations of Monarchical splendor, aided by the countenance and encouragement of the great and opulent.

S 2                    SECTION

# SECTION V.

## THAT

## ORIGINAL POETIC

## G E N I U S

Will in general be difplayed in its utmoft Vigour

### IN THE EARLY AND UNCULTIVATED

## PERIODS of SOCIETY

Which are peculiarly favourable to it;

### AND THAT

It will feldom appear in a very high Degree in

## CULTIVATED LIFE.

HAVING pointed out the exertions of ORIGINAL GENIUS in the different Arts, and particularly in Poetry, we fhall now confider the period of fociety moft favourable

vourable to the diſplay of ORIGINALITY of GENIUS in the laſt mentioned art; and this period we affirm to be the earlieſt and leaſt cultivated.

To aſſert that this divine art, to an ex-cellence in which the higheſt efforts of hu-man Genius are requiſite, ſhould attain its utmoſt perfection in the infancy of ſociety, when mankind are only emerging from a ſtate of ignorance and barbarity, will appear a paradox to ſome, though it is an unques-tionable truth; and a cloſer attention will convince us, that it is agreeable to reaſon, as well as confirmed by experience.

While Arts and Sciences are in their firſt rude and imperfect ſtate, there is great ſcope afforded for the exertions of Genius. Much is to be obſerved; much is to be diſ-covered and invented. Imagination how-ever in general exerts itſelf with more ſucceſs in the Arts than in the Sciences; in the for-mer of which its ſucceſs is more rapid than

S 3

in

in the latter. Active as this faculty is in its operations, its discoveries in science are for the most part attained by slow and gradual steps. They are the effect of long and severe investigation ; and receive their highest improvement in the most civilized state of society. On the other hand the efforts of Imagination, in Poetry at least, are impetuous, and attain their utmost perfection at once, even in the rudest form of social life. This art does not require long and sedulous application, to confer Originality and excellence on its productions : its earliest unlaboured essays generally possess both in the highest degree. The reasons why they do so, will be assigned immediately. In the mean time we may observe, as a circumstance deserving our attention, that this is by no means the case with the other arts, but is peculiar to Poetry alone. Painting, Eloquence, Music and Architecture, attain their highest improvement by the repeated efforts of ingenious Artists, as well as the sciences by the reiterated researches and ex-

periments

periments of Philofophers; though, as we have already obferved, Imagination operates with greater rapidity in the improvement of the former, than in that of the latter; but ftill it operates gradually in the improvement of both. There never arofe an eminent Painter, Orator, Mufician, Architect or Philofopher, in any age, completely felf-taught, without being indebted to his predeceffors in the art or fcience he profeffed. Should it be objected, that the art of Painting was revived, and brought to the utmoft perfection to which it ever arrived in modern times, in one fingle age, that of Leo the Tenth, we anfwer, That the *Italian* Mafters, though they had none of the ancient paintings to ferve them as models, had however fome admirable remains both of the *Grecian* and *Roman* ftatuary, which, by heightening their ideas of excellence in its fifter art, and kindling their ambition, contributed greatly to the perfection of their works. Arts and Sciences indeed generally rife and fall together; but, excepting Poetry

S 4                           alone,

alone; they rife and fall by juft, though
not always by equal degrees: fometimes advancing with quicker progrefs to the fummit
of excellence, fometimes declining from it
by flower fteps; in proportion to the different degrees of Genius, and application with
which they are cultivated, confidered in
connection with thofe external caufes, which
promote or obftruct their improvement.
It is very remarkable however, that in the
earlieft and moft uncultivated periods of
fociety, Poetry is by one great effort of nature, in one age, and by one individual,
brought to the higheft perfection to which
human Genius is capable of advancing it;
not only when the other Arts and Sciences
are in a languifhing ftate, but when they
do not fo much as exift. Thus HOMER
wrote his *Iliad* and *Odyſſey*, when there
was not a fingle picture to be feen in
*Greece*; and OSSIAN compofed *Fingal* and
*Temora*, when none of the Arts, whether
liberal or mechanical, were known in his
country. This is a curious phenomenon;

non ; let us endeavour to account for it.

The firſt reaſon we ſhall aſſign of ORIGI-NAL POETIC GENIUS being moſt remarkably diſplayed in an early and uncultivated period of ſociety, ariſes from the antiquity of the period itſelf, and from the appearance of novelty in the objects which Genius contemplates. A Poet of real Genius, who lives in a diſtant uncultivated age, poſſeſſes great and peculiar advantages for original compoſition, by the mere antiquity of the period in which he lives. He is perhaps the firſt Poet who hath ariſen in this infant ſtate of ſociety ; by which means he enjoys the undivided empire of Imagination without a rival. The mines of Fancy not having been opened before his time, are left to be digged by him ; and the treaſures they contain become his own, by a right derived from the firſt diſcovery. The whole ſyſtem of nature, and the whole region of fiction, yet unexplored by others, is ſubjected to his

ſurvey,

furvey, from which he culls thofe rich fpoils, which adorn his compofitions, and render them original. It may be faid indeed, in anfwer to this, and it is true, That the ftores of nature are inexhauftible by human imagination, and that her face is ever various and ever new; but it may be replied, That fome of her ftores are more readily found than others, being lefs hid from the eye of Fancy, and fome of her features more eafily hit, becaufe more ftrongly marked. The firft good Poet therefore, poffeffing thofe unrifled treafures, and contemplating thefe unfullied features, could not fail to prefent us with a draught fo ftriking, as to deferve the name of a complete ORIGINAL. We may farther obferve, that the objects with which he is furrounded, have an appearance of novelty, which, in a more cultivated period, they in a great meafure lofe; but which, in that we are fpeaking of, excites an attention, curiofity and furprife, highly favourable to the exertion of Genius, and fomewhat refembling

that

Straight toward Heaven my wond'ring eyes I turn'd,
And gaz'd a while the ample fky.

*Paradife Loft*, Book viii. line 257.

    About me round I faw
Hill, dale, and fhady woods, and funny plains,
And liquid lapfe of murmuring ftreams.

        *Line* 261.

Such a perfon looks round him with wonder; every object is new to him, and has
the power to affect him with furprife and
pleafure; and as he is not familiarifed by
previous defcription to the fcenes he contemplates, thefe ftrike upon his mind with
their full force; and the Imagination afto-
niflied and enraptured with the furvey of
the Vaft, the Wild, and the Beautiful in
nature, conveyed through the medium of
fenfe, fpontaneoufly expreffes its vivid ideas
in bold and glowing metaphors, in fublime,
animated and picturefque defcription. Even
           a Poet

a Poet of ordinary Genius will in such a
state of society present us with some original ideas in his compositions; for nature
lying open to his view in all its extent and
variety, in contemplating this unbounded
field, so small a part of which hath been
yet occupied by others, he can hardly fail to
select some distinguishing objects which have
escaped the notice of the vulgar, and which
described in Poetry may stamp upon it a degree of ORIGINALITY.

We may add, that the productions of
the early ages, when they present to us
scenes of nature and a state of life we are
little acquainted with, and which are very
different from those that now subsist, will
to us appear original, though they may not
be really such if the true originals are lost,
of which the works that yet remain are
only copies or imitations. Thus the Co-
medies of TERENCE are valued, because the
Originals of MENANDER, which the *Roman*
Poet imitated, excepting a few fragments,
                                                        are

are loft. Could the works of the latter be
recovered, thofe of the former would lofe
much of their reputation. Thus far the
fuperiority of Poetic Genius in thofe early
ages is accidental, and therefore no way
meritorious. It is the effect of a particular fituation. It is the confequence of antiquity.

The next reafon we fhall give, why original Poetic Genius appears in its utmoft perfection in the firft periods of focial life, is
the fimplicity and uniformity of manners
peculiar to fuch periods.

Manners have a much greater effect on
the exertions of Poetic Genius, than is
commonly imagined. The fimple manners
which prevail among moft nations in the
infancy of fociety, are peculiarly favourable
to fuch exertions. In this primitive ftate of
nature, when mankind begin to unite in
fociety, the manners, fentiments, and paffions are (if we may ufe the expreffion)
perfectly

perfectly ORIGINAL. They are the dictates of nature, unmixed and undisguised : they are therefore more easily comprehended and described. The Poet in describing his own feelings, describes also the feelings of others; for in such a state of society, these are similar and uniform in all. Their tastes, dispositions, and manners are thrown into the same mould, and generally formed upon one and the same model. Artless and tender loves, generous friendships, and warlike exploits, compose the history of this uncultivated period; and the Poet who relates these, feeling the inspiration of his subject, is himself animated with all the ardor of the Lover, the Friend, and the Hero. Hence as his sensations are warm and vivid, his sentiments will become passionate or sublime, as the occasion may require; his descriptions energetic; his stile bold, elevated, and metaphorical; and the whole, being the effusion of a glowing fancy and an impassioned heart, will be perfectly natural and ORIGINAL. Thus far

far then an early and uncultivated ftate of fociety, in which the manners, fentiments and paffions, run in the uniform current above-mentioned (as they do in moft infant focieties) appears favourable to the difplay of original Poetic Genius.

A third caufe of this quality's being remarkably exerted in an early period of fociety, is the leifure and tranquillity of uncultivated life, together with the innocent pleafures which generally attend it.

GENIUS naturally fhoots forth in the fimplicity and tranquillity of uncultivated life. The undifturbed peace, and the innocent rural pleafures of this primeval ftate, are, if we may fo exprefs it, congenial to its nature. A Poet of true Genius delights to contemplate and defcribe thofe primitive fcenes, which recal to our remembrance the fabulous era of the golden age. Happily exempted from that tormenting ambition, and thofe vexatious defires, which trouble the

the current of modern life, he wanders with a ferene, contented heart, through walks and groves confecrated to the Mufes; or, indulging a fublime, penfive, and fweetly-foothing melancholy, ftrays with a flow and folemn ftep, through the unfrequented de-fert, along the naked beach, or the bleak and barren heath. In fuch a fituation, every theme is a fource of infpiration, whether he defcribes the beauties of na-ture, which he furveys with tranfport; or the peaceful innocence of thofe happy times, which are fo wonderfully foothing and pleafing to the imagination. His defcrip-tions therefore will be perfectly vivid and original, becaufe they are the tranfcript of his own feelings. Such a fituation as that we have above reprefented, is particularly favourable to a paftoral Poet, and is very fimilar to that enjoyed by THEOCRITUS, which no doubt had a happy influence on his compofitions; and it is a fituation highly propitious to the efforts of every fpecies of Poetic Genius.

Perhaps

Perhaps we may be thought to refine too much on this point; and it may be questioned whether such tranquillity and innocence as we have above suppofed have ever existed in any state of society. To this we may anfwer, That though the traditionary or even hiftorical accounts of the early ages, are not much to be depended on; yet thofe ancient original poems which we have in our hands, give us reafon to think that a certain innocence of manners, accompanied with that tranquillity which is its confequence, prevailed among thofe people whom we are not afhamed to call barbarous, in a much higher degree than in more modern and cultivated periods.

The laft caufe we fhall affign why original Poetic Genius appears in its utmoft perfection in the uncultivated ages of fociety, is, its exemption from the rules and reftraints of Criticifm, and its want of that knowledge which is acquired from books. When we confider learning and critical

knowledge

knowledge as unfavourable to original Poetry, we hope we shall not be accused of pleading the cause of ignorance, rusticity, and barbarism; any more than when we speak of the happy influence of the simple uncultivated periods of society on the productions of the above-mentioned art, we shall be supposed to prefer those rude and artless ages to a highly civilized state of life. The effects of Literature and Criticism in the improvement of all the sciences and all the arts, excepting Poetry alone; and the advantages of a state of civilization, in augmenting and refining the pleasures of social life, are too obvious to require to be pointed out. We are at present only concerned to examine the effects of Learning and critical Knowledge on original Poetry, the want of which we affirm to be one of the principal causes of this art's being carried to its highest perfection in the first uncultivated periods of human society.

Let

Let us inquire into the effects of thefe, upon the mind of a Poet poffeffed of a high degree of original Genius. By an acquaintance with that Literature which is derived from books, it will be granted, he may attain the knowledge of a great variety of events, and fee human nature in a great variety of forms. By collecting the obfervations and experience of paft ages, by fuperadding his own, and by reafoning juftly from acknowledged principles, he may, no doubt, acquire more accurate and extenfive ideas of the works of Nature and Art, and may likewife be thereby qualified to inrich the Sciences with new difcoveries, as well as moft of the Arts with new inventions and improvements. In his own art only he can never become an original Author by fuch means; nor, ftrictly fpeaking, fo much as acquire the materials, by the ufe of which he may juftly attain this character: for the ideas derived from books, that is, from the ideas of others, can by no procefs of poetical chymiftry confer perfect Originality.

T 2      Thofe

Thofe ideas which are the intire creation of
the mind, or are the refult of the Poet's
own obfervations, and immediately drawn
from nature, are the only original ones in
the proper fenfe.  A Poet who adopts
images, who culls out incidents he has met
with in the writings of other Authors, and
who imitates characters which have been
portrayed by other Poets, or perhaps by
Hiftorians, cannot furely with any propriety
be confidered as an Original, though he may
at the fame time difcover confiderable powers
of Imagination in adapting thofe images and
incidents, as well as transforming and mold-
ing thefe characters to the general defign of
his poem.  In order to become a Poet perfectly original (of whom only it muft be
remembered we are here treating) he muft,
if he fhould attempt Epic Poetry, invent
images, incidents and characters : tradition
may indeed fupply him with the groundwork
of the poem, as it did HOMER, but the fuperftructure muft be altogether his own.
In executing fuch a work, what aid can a
truly

truly original Poet receive from books? If
he borrows aid from the performances of
others, he is no longer a complete Original.
To maintain this character throughout, he
muſt rely on his own fund: his own plaſtic imagination muſt ſupply him with every
thing.

But ſuch intire Originality very rarely
happens, eſpecially in a modern age. Many
of the moſt ſplendid images of Poetry have
been already exhibited, many of the moſt
ſtriking characters in human life have been
delineated, and many of the moſt beautiful
objects of nature, and ſuch as are moſt obvious, have been deſcribed by preceding
Bards. It will be very difficult therefore for
their ſucceſſors to ſelect objects which the
eye of Fancy hath never explored, and none
but a Genius uncommonly original can hope
to accompliſh it.

There are very different degrees of Originality in Poetry; and ſeveral eminent Geniuſes

niufes in this art, poffeffing a very confiderable fhare of Originality themfelves, have
however been contented to imitate the great
Father of Epic Poetry in one circumftance
or another; partly perhaps through a con-
fciouinefs of their being unable to produce
any thing of a different kind equal to his
compofitions, partly through a natural tendency to imitate the excellencies they admired
in a model rendered venerable by the con-
current teftimonies of all ages in his favour,
and partly through the real difficulty of attaining complete Originality in the province
of the *Epopœa* after him. Thus VIRGIL
copied many of the epifodes and images of
the *Mæonian* Bard; TASSO imitated fome of
his characters, as well as adopted a part of
his imagery; and even the divine MILTON
condefcended, in a very few inftances indeed, to imitate this Prince of ancient Poets,
in cafes where his own Genius, left to its
native energy, and uninfluenced by an acquaintance with the Writings of HOMER,
would have enabled him to equal the *Greek*
Poet.

Poet. An inftance of this kind occurs in the end of the fourth book of *Paradife Loft*, where MILTON informs us that Satan, while he was preparing for a dreadful combat with his antagonift, fled away, upon obferving that one of the fcales which were fufpended from Heaven, kicked the beam, thereby prefaging to him an unfortunate iffue of the encounter. By this cool expedient, which was fuggefted by that paffage of HOMER, in which JUPITER is fuppofed to weigh the fates of HECTOR and ACHILLES in his golden balance, MILTON has prevented the confequences of this horrid fray, facrificed a real excellence to a frivolous imitation, and very much difappointed the eager expectations of the Reader. The Poet's own Genius, had he been unacquainted with the *Iliad*, would naturally have led him to defcribe thofe mighty combatants engaged in dreadful fight; but a propenfity to the imitation of fo eminent an Author, repreffed the native ardor of his own imagination. This fingle inftance is fufficient to fhew us the

effect

effect of Literature on the mind of a Poet
of original Genius, whofe exertions it probably will in fome inftances fupprefs, but
cannot in any inftance affift.   On the other
hand, a Poet living in the more early periods of fociety, having few or no preceding
Bards for his models, is in very little hazard
of being betrayed into imitation, which in a
modern age it is fo difficult to avoid ; but,
giving full fcope to the bent of his Genius,
he is enabled, if he is poffeffed of a high degree of this quality, to produce a Work
completely original.   From this train of
reafoning it appears, that the Literature
which is acquired from books, efpecially
from the Works of preceding Bards, is unfavourable to Originality in Poetry ; and
that Poets who live in the firft periods
of fociety, who are deftitute of the means
of learning, and confequently are exempted from the poffibility of Imitation, en-
joy peculiar advantages for original compofition.

We

We may add, that another effect of learning is, to ENCUMBER and OVERLOAD the mind of an original Poetic Genius. Indeed it has this effect upon the mind of every man who has not properly arranged its scattered materials, and who by thought and reflection has not "digested into sense the motley meal †." But however properly arranged those materials may be, and however thoroughly digested this intellectual food, an original Genius will sometimes find an inconveniency resulting from it; for as no man can attend to and comprehend many different things at once, his mental faculties will in some cases be necessarily oppressed and overcharged with the immensity of his own conceptions, when weighed down by the additional load of learning. The truth is, a Poet of original Genius has very little occasion for the weak aid of Literature: he is self-taught. He comes into the world as it were completely accomplished. Nature sup-

---

† *Night Thoughts.*

plies

plies the materials of his compofitions; his fenfes are the under-workmen, while Imagination, like a mafterly Architect, fuperintends and directs the whole. Or, to fpeak more properly, Imagination both fupplies the materials, and executes the work, fince it calls into being " things that are not," and creates and peoples worlds of its own. It may be eafily conceived therefore, that an original Poetic Genius, poffeffing fuch innate treafure (if we may be allowed an unphilofophical expreffion) has no ufe for that which is derived from books, fince he may be encumbered, but cannot be inriched by it; for though the chief merit of ordinary Writers may confift in arranging and prefenting us with the thoughts of others, that of an original Writer will always confift in prefenting us with fuch thoughts as are his own.

We obferved likewife, that an EXEMPTION from the RULES and RESTRAINTS of CRITI-CISM, contributed greatly to the more remarkable difplay of original Poetic Genius in the

the firft ages of fociety. Every fpecies of original Genius delights to range at liberty, and efpecially original Poetic Genius, which abhors the fetters of Criticifm, claims the privilege of the freeborn fons of Nature, and never relinquifhes it without the utmoft regret. This noble talent knows no law, and acknowledges none in the uncultivated ages of the world, excepting its own fpontaneous impulfe, which it obeys without control, and without any dread of the cenfure of Critics. The truth is, Criticifm was never formed into a fyftem, till ARISTOTLE, that penetrating, and (to ufe an expreffion by which VOLTAIRE characterifes Mr LOCKE) " methodical Genius" arofe, who deduced his Poetics, not from his own imagination, but from his accurate obfervations on the Works of HOMER, SOPHOCLES, ÆSCHYLUS, and EURIPIDES. Let us obferve the probable and natural effects which a ftrict adherence to the rules of Criticifm will have on original Genius in Poetry. One obvious effect of it is, that it confines the attention to artificial rules, and

ties

ties the mind down to the obſervance of them, perhaps at the very time that the imagination is upon the ſtretch, and graſping at ſome idea aſtoniſhingly great, which however it is obliged, though with the utmoſt reluctance, to quit, being intimidated by the apprehen- ſion of incurring cenſure. By this means, the irregular but noble boldneſs of Fancy is checked, the divine and impetuous ardor of Genius is, we do not ſay extinguiſhed, but in a great meaſure ſuppreſſed, and many ſhining excellencies ſacrificed to juſtneſs of deſign, and regular uniformity of execution.

The candid Reader will obſerve, that the queſtion we have been examining is not whether critical Learning be upon the whole really uſeful to an Author of Genius, ſo as to render his Works more perfect and accurate, but what its particular effect will be upon the productions of a Genius truly original. We are far from intending to diſregard or cenſure thoſe rules " for writing well," which have been eſtabliſhed by ſound judgment, and

and an exact difcernment of the various fpecies of compofition; an attempt that would
be equally weak and vain. On the contrary,
we profefs a reverence for thofe laws of writing, which good fenfe and the correfponding
voice of ages have pronounced important;
and we confider them as what ought never
to be violated; though with refpect to others
of a more trivial nature, however binding
they may be upon ordinary Authors, we can
look upon them in no other light, than as
the frivolous fetters of original Genius, to
which it has fubmitted through fear, always
improperly, and fometimes ridiculoufly, but
which it may boldly fhake off at pleafure; at
leaft whenever it finds them fuppreffing its
exertion, or whenever it can reach an uncommon excellence by its emancipation.

Upon the whole, from the reafons above
affigned, it feems evident, that the EARLY
UNCULTIVATED ages of fociety are moft favourable to the difplay of original Genius in
Poetry; whence it is natural to expect, that

in

in fuch ages the greateft Originals in this
art will always arife. Unhappily for us, this
point does not admit of proof from an induction of many particulars; for very few
original Poems of thofe nations among whom
they might have been expected, have defcend-
ed through the viciffitudes and revolutions of
fo many ages to our times. Moft of the monuments of Genius, as well as the works of
Art, have perifhed in the general wreck of
empire; and we can only conjecture the merit
of fuch as are loft from that of the fmall
number of thofe which remain. While the
Works of HOMER and OSSIAN however are
in our hands, thefe, without any other examples, will be fufficient to eftablifh the truth
of the firft part of our affertion, That in the
early periods of fociety, original Poetic Genius
will in general be exerted in its utmoft vigour. Let us now proceed to fhew the truth
of the fecond part of it, which was, That
this quality will feldom appear in a very high
degree in cultivated life, and let us affign the
reafons of it.

SHAKESPEAR

SHAKESPEAR is the only modern Author, (whose times by the way compared with the present are not very modern) whom, in point of Originality, we can venture to compare with those eminent ancient Poets above-mentioned. In sublimity of Genius indeed, MILTON is inferior to neither of them; but it cannot be pretended that he was so complete an Original as the one or the other, since he was indebted to the sacred Writings for several important incidents, and for many sublime sentiments, to be met with in *Paradise Lost*; not to mention what was formerly observed, that in a few passages he imitated the great Father of Poetry. With respect to SHAKESPEAR therefore, admitting him to be a modern Author, he is at any rate but a single exception; though indeed his Genius was so strangely irregular, and so different from that of every other Mortal, *Cui nihil simile aut secundum*, that no argument can be drawn from such an example to invalidate our position; since he would probably have discovered the same great and eccentric Genius,

which

which we fo much admire at prefent, in any
age or country whatever.  External caufes,
though they have great influence on common
minds, would have had very little on fuch a
one as SHAKESPEAR's.  Let it be confeffed,
however, in juftice to our own age, that if
it hath not produced fuch perfect Originals
as thofe above-mentioned, which perhaps
may be partly imputed to the influence of
caufes peculiar to the prefent period and ftate
of fociety, yet it hath produced feveral elegant, and fome exalted Geniufes in Poetry ;
who are diftinguifhed alfo by a very confiderable degree of Originality, and fuch as is
rarely to be met with in a modern age. The
names of YOUNG, GRAY, OGILVIE, COLLINS,
AKENSIDE, and MASON, as they do honour
to the prefent age, will probably be tranf-
mitted with reputation to pofterity.  But
fince it muft be univerfally allowed, that fuch
intire Originality, as we have fhewn to be
competent to an uncultivated period, hath
never yet appeared in modern times, excepting in the fingle inftance above-mentioned,

it

it may be worth the while to inquire into the caufes why it fo feldom appears, or can be expected to appear in cultivated life.

If we have fuccefsfully inveftigated the caufes why original Poetic Genius is moft re-markably difplayed in the uncultivated ftate of fociety; we fhall probably difcover that the chief caufes of its being rarely found in the fame degree in more civilized ages, are the OPPOSITES of the former. Thus the firft caufe we affigned of this quality's being exerted in a higher degree in the EARLIER periods of focial life, was deduced from the ANTIQUITY of thofe periods, and the SMALL PROGRESS of CULTIVATION in them. One reafon therefore why it will fo feldom appear in a later period, muft be the difadvantage of living fo long after the field of Fancy hath been preoccupied by the more ancient Bards. We have already allowed that a truly origi-nal Poet will ftrike out a path for himfelf; but it muft likewife be allowed, that to do fo after his illuftrious predeceffors, will at leaft

U                                         be

be more difficult. To what hath been above advanced on this head, we fhall here only add a fingle obfervation, that fhould any modern Poet with juftice claim an equality ot merit with the renowned Ancients in point of Originality, he would, confidering the difadvantages he muft labour undei, be intitled to a ftill fuperior fhare of reputation. In the mean time we may reafonably infer, that the difference in the period of fociety abovementioned, will always prove unfavourable to the Originality of a modern Poet; and may be confidered as one caufe why this quality rarely appears in a very high degree in polifhed life.

We confidered the SIMPLICITY and UNIFORMITY of ancient Manners, as another caufe why original Genius is exerted in its utmoft vigour in the FIRST periods of fociety. We may remark, on the other hand, that the DIVERSITY, DISSIPATION, and exceffive REFINEMENTS of modern Manners, will naturally prove unfavourable to its exertion,

in

in later and more civilized ages. Where
there is a great diverfity of Manners, it will
be difficult to mark and to defcribe the predominating colours. Where Diffipation pre-
vails, Genius is in danger of being drawn
within its vortex ; and the falfe refinements
in Luxury and Pleafure, which are characteriftical of later ages, though they are confiftent enough with, and even productive of
the improvement of all the mechanical, and
fome of the liberal Arts; yet they are un-
friendly to the two moft fublime of all the
liberal Arts, original Poetry and Eloquence.
An excefs of Luxury is indeed almoft as unfavourable to the cultivation of Genius in
thefe, as it is to the cultivation of Virtue. It
enfeebles the mind, as it corrupts the heart,
and gradually fuppreffes that ftrenuous exertion of the mental faculties, by which confummate excellence is to be attained. Poetic
Genius in particular cannot flourifh either
in uninterrupted SUNSHINE, or in continual
SHADE. It languifhes under the blazing ardor of a fummer noon, as its buds are blafted

by

by the damp fogs and chilling breath of a winter sky. Poverty is scarce more unfavourable to the display of true Poetic Genius than exceffive Affluence is. The former crushes its early and aspiring efforts at once; the latter more flowly, but no lefs furely, enervates its powers, and diffolves them in Luxury and Pleafure. It was a fensible observation of a *French* Monarch *, though the conjunction be fomewhat fantaftical, *Poetæ & equi alendi, non faginandi*. The fituation moft defirable for a Poet is the middle ftate of life. He ought neither to riot in the fulnefs of opulence, nor to feel the pinching wants of poverty, but to poffefs that eafe and independence, which are neceffary to unfold the bloffoms of Genius to the utmoft advantage.

The third caufe which we affigned of original Poetic Genius being moft remarkably difplayed in the uncultivated ftate of fo-

---

* CHARLES the Ninth.

ciety,

ciety, was the LEISURE and TRANQUILLITY naturally refulting from fuch a ftate. The caufe therefore why it feldom appears in a more advanced period, will be juft the re-verfe of the former, namely, the ACTIVITY and ARDOR, the HURRY and BUSTLE obferv-able in modern ages, occafioned by their eager purfuits, and the clafhing interefts of mankind. As the voice of Confcience is often drowned amidft the clamours of tu-multuous paffion, fo the flame of Genius is frequently fmothered by the bufy, buftling cares of an active life. The thorny path of Ambition, and the painful, patient purfuit of Gain, are both unfavourable, though not in an equal degree, to its native ardor. The former occafions a diftraction, harafsment, and anxiety of thought; the latter an intire depreffion of the powers of Imagination. Genius is mifled by the one, perverted by the other. Indeed it fcarce ever happens, that a high degree of this quality is allied to Avarice: it feldom ftoops to the drudgery of laborious bufinefs for the fake of wealth, of
which

which it is naturally very little folicitous, and with the ardent defire of which it is in a great meafure incompatible. Ambition however has charms capable of feducing it. Honour and Power are objects at which it frequently afpires; and they often prove obftructions to its native exertions in its proper fphere, by engaging the mind in purfuits, which produce embarrassment and perplexity. True Genius, removed from the din and tumult of bufinefs and care, fhoots up to the nobleft height; it fpreads forth all its luxuriance in the peaceful vale of rural tranquillity. Its fate in advanced fociety, and amidft the croud of mankind, is very different. There it meets with many obftacles to check its progrefs, and to difcourage its efforts. Expofed to the affaults of malignity and envy, it falls the victim of unmerited calumny; or, intangled in thofe vexatious purfuits which interrupt the repofe of mankind, its ardor is wafted in the tumultuous career of ambition, and its powers abforbed in the unfathomable gulf of fenfual indulgence.

The

The laſt cauſe we took notice of as favourable to original Poetry in ancient times, while ſociety was yet in its rudeſt form, was the WANT of LITERATURE, and an EXEMPTION from the RULES of CRITICISM. It will follow therefore by juſt conſequence, that the acquaintance with LITERATURE and CRITICAL KNOWLEDGE, which is ſo conſiderably diffuſed in modern times, muſt be equally unfavourable to the exertion of original Poetic Genius in thoſe times.

Having conſidered the effect of theſe accompliſhments upon the mind of an original Poet at great length, in the former part of this ſection, we ſhall conclude with a remark, which will exhibit in one view the ſubſtance of what hath been more fully diſcuſſed in the preceding pages. It is, that though the progreſs of Literature, Criticiſm and Civilization, have contributed to unfold the powers and extend the empire of Reaſon; have taught men to think more juſtly, as well as to expreſs their ſentiments with more preciſion;

fion; have had the happieft influence on the Arts and Sciences in general (fince by communicating the difcoveries, inventions, and obfervations of preceding ages, they have facilitated the way to future inventions and difcoveries, and have been highly conducive to their improvement) yet the art of original Poetry, to an excellence in which the wild exuberance and plaftic force of Genius are the only requifites, hath fuffered, inftead of having gained, from the influence of the above-mentioned caufes; and will, for the moft part, be difplayed in its utmoft perfection in the early and uncultivated periods of focial life.

THE END.